NEW MEXICO EPISODES

Stories from a Colorful Past

NEW MEXICO EPISODES

Stories from a Colorful Past

John Philip Wilson

SUNSTONE
PRESS
SANTA FE

Sunstone books may be purchased for educational, business, or sales promotional use. For information please write: Special Markets Department, Sunstone Press, P.O. Box 2321, Santa Fe, New Mexico 87504-2321.

Book and cover design › R. Ahl
Printed on acid-free paper
∞
eBook 978-1-61139-595-2

———————————————

Library of Congress Cataloging-in-Publication Data

Names: Wilson, John P. (John Philip), 1935- author.
Title: New Mexico episodes : stories from a colorful past / by John Philip Wilson.
Description: Santa Fe, New Mexico : Sunstone Press, [2020] | Includes bibliographical references. | Summary: "A collection of true episodes from Spanish-Colonial New Mexico to the twentieth century, involving both the little-known and the well-known"-- Provided by publisher.
Identifiers: LCCN 2020025266 | ISBN 9781632933041 (paperback) | ISBN 9781611395952 (epub) | ISBN 1632933047 (paperback)
Subjects: LCSH: New Mexico--History--Anecdotes.
Classification: LCC F796.6 .W55 2020 | DDC 978.9--dc23
LC record available at https://lccn.loc.gov/2020025266

———————————————

WWW.SUNSTONEPRESS.COM
SUNSTONE PRESS / POST OFFICE BOX 2321 / SANTA FE, NM 87504-2321 /USA
(505) 988-4418 / FAX (505) 988-1025

DEDICATION

For Albert H. Schroeder, long-time National Park Service archaeologist and researcher, who inspired others.

CONTENTS

~ PREFACE ~

THIRTEEN EPISODES IN NEW MEXICO'S LONG HISTORY ARE EXPLORED HERE to give insights into the wide variety of events that helped weave the rich tapestry of this state's past. We meet the very first European explorer and learn something of what he was told by the natives. Later we learn what became of a settler's house that still bore his name two hundred years after he left it. After 1846, miners, ranchers and others began to explore the country away from the Rio Grande and, within a generation, travelers were crossing the territory via stagecoach while occasionally being the victims of "knights of the road," who made their living by preying on passengers.

The military played an important role in nineteenth century New Mexico, and we see something of what life was like at a Civil War-era Army post, as well as glimpsing southeastern New Mexico when its only inhabitants were Apache Indians. Even in the settled areas, systems we now take for granted such as mail delivery and communicating with the world outside were handled very differently than today.

Little-known aspects of New Mexico's best-known badman, Billy the Kid, still lurk in the byways of the past, while for those not already familiar with it, the controversial and bloody history of the year-long conflict known as the Lincoln County War is sketched out. Nor was this violence unique to Lincoln County, as an account from Grant County in western New Mexico shows. Much later, during World War I, an enemy saboteur working for Emperor Franz-Joseph I of Austria-Hungary was apprehended by a U.S. Forest Service ranger. And like all good anthologies, there is a dog story.

These chapters came together at the suggestion of a good friend and highly-respected historian, Dr. Harwood Hinton. Early in 1985, after I received a contract with a state agency to write a history of the Lincoln County War, I decided to begin my research by reviewing the Maurice Fulton Papers now housed at the University of Arizona Special Collections Library. At that time Dr. Hinton, whom I did not know, had an office in the main library building. He customarily swooped down to the special collections reading room and took whatever scholars were at work there to lunch at the faculty dining rooms across the campus. I was one of the swoopees and very much enjoyed the companionship and conversations, as well as the lunches.

I told him that I was at a loss to know how I should orient my history of this already-overwritten subject. Harwood, who was most familiar with it from his own research, said "Well, you know what they said about [President] Nixon—follow the money!" That struck me, and that was what I did—the Lincoln County War as a battle for economic dominance!

A decade or so later, I was back in Tucson for another project and mentioned to Harwood that I had no good ideas for another writing project. This time he said, why don't you compile some of the non-fiction stories that you've scattered here and there, mostly in journals or newsletters that historians usually don't see, rewrite these and make them into a book? Again, a suggestion worth considering. Several years later, after I had retired, I took him up on this idea. The present book is one of the results!

How all of these chapters came to be written is a different story for each. The one about the saboteur originated with a reminiscence by former ranger Elliott Barker, published in a three-volume Forest Service compilation called *The Early Days: Books 1-3*. The story about the seventeenth-century settler Felipe Romero grew out of my reading the testimonies in the Sevilleta Land Grant microfilm, which I had been searching for any references to archaeological remains. The Lincoln County War and Billy the Kid articles are spin-offs from my 1987 book, *Merchants, Guns & Money*. The Fort McRae piece and Captain Claiborne's report had their start when I spotted the brief journal and various accounts of Army scouting parties among the documents in the Schroeder Collection at the New Mexico State Records Center and Archives.

Some of the other articles derive from my reading countless microfilms of nineteenth-century New Mexico newspapers. The Marata chapter is based upon my website about the kingdom of Marata, which in turn grew out of my disappointment with both historians and archaeologists about their lack of any effort to confirm the existence of such a site, whose general location had been cited by the friar Marcos de Niza but never actually visited. Finding Marata turned out to be fairly straightforward, and the Zuni Indian traditions about it (under different names), as recorded by early-day anthropologists, fell into place. Its walls still stood four feet high in the 1880s.

There are no necessary connections between any of these short narratives. They were drafted originally over a period of almost forty years, and about half have not been previously published. For the most part, acknowledgements are owing to Drs. Hinton and Albert H. Schroeder, with thanks also to the rancher who allowed me to complete my mapping of the Marata ruin.

The articles that have seen print before are rewritten here, sometimes with many changes and additions from the original drafts. Readers are invited to pick and choose; the texts are of various lengths and, as said, cover a wide variety of topics. For the most part, they have been chosen to represent aspects of New Mexico's history not explored elsewhere. They are given here as entertainment and perhaps will inspire others to do new research, which in turn may help flesh out what we already know. I hope that they appeal to anyone with an interest in New Mexico history. Original research is always a challenge, but it can be immensely rewarding.

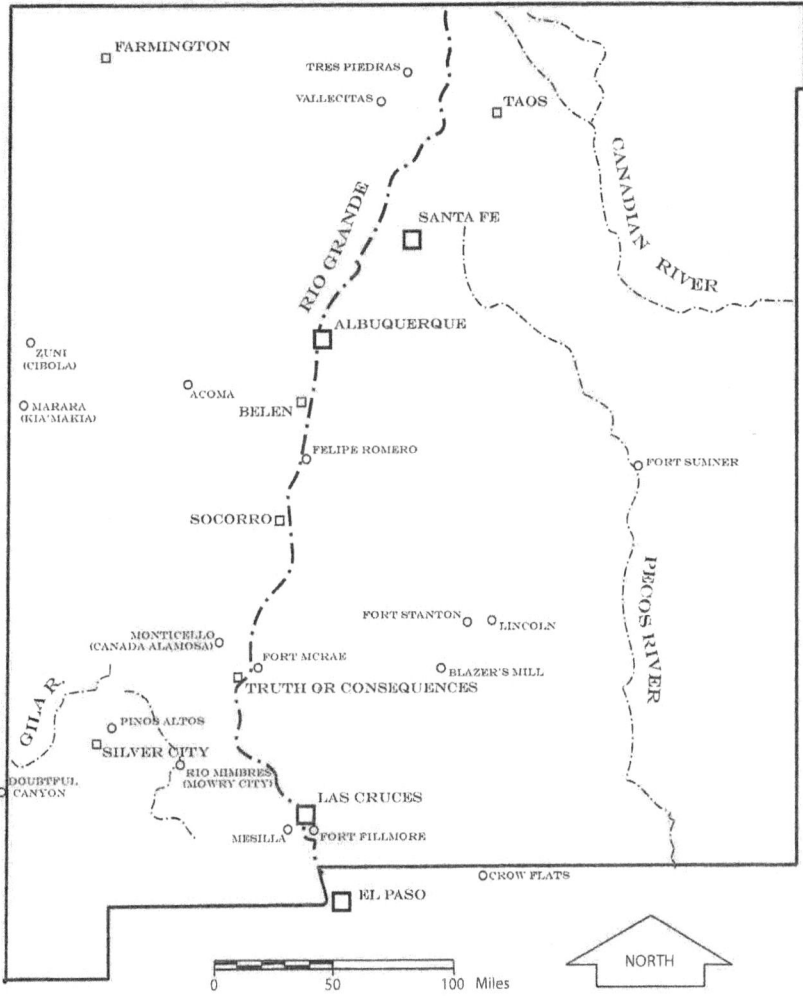

1. Some Locations for *New Mexico Episodes*. Map by the author.

~ 1 ~

MARATA, A NEW MEXICO KINGDOM

(WITH NOTES ON TOTONTEAC)

IN THE SPRING OF 1539, ANTONIO DE MENDOZA, THE VICEROY OF NEW SPAIN, sent the Franciscan friar Marcos de Niza on a mission to find a route northward beyond the settled limits of New Spain. He was to determine the nature of the lands and the people, and to gather information about the western coastline. Fray Marcos set off, and after passing the last Spanish settlements he sent one of his companions, Esteban de Dorantes, in advance to see if a rich and settled land might lie beyond.

Within days, Esteban sent back word that thirty days ahead lay seven very great *ciudades* or cities, ruled by a single lord. The first and greatest was called Cibola. He had talked with natives who told him that besides the seven cities, there were three other *reinos* or kingdoms called Maratta, Acus, and Totonteac. These names were all new and no maps of the period showed their locations. Fray Marcos was still well down in modern Sonora.

The priest continued four days through a *despoblado* or unoccupied region that would probably have included the San Rafael Valley in southern Arizona. Soon he arrived at a heavily settled area with clusters of houses a mile or so apart. While he gave no name to this place or its people, a modern estimate is that he was now in the San Pedro Valley of southern Arizona, among the Indians known later as Sobaipuris.

These people gave the good father a wealth of information about the seven cities. Even before this, Indians had shown him shields made of *cueros de vaca,* or cow-hides, which came from Cibola. These cow-hides were the skins of bison which in the Zuni Indian language are called *ciwolos*. In Spanish, this became *cibolos* or *civolos,* and the name came into use for the whole province of Cibola.

An elderly native, an exile from Cibola, told Fray Marcos that:

...to the southeast (of Cibola) there is a *reino* called Maratta in which there used to be many very grand settlements. They all have these [same] multistoried houses made of stone. These [people] have been and are at war with the lord of these seven *ciudades.* Because of this war the *reino* of Maratta has shrunk to a great extent. It still rules itself, however, and is at war with these other *reinos.*

An alternative translation of the last sentence by philologist Jerry Craddock reads:

This Kingdom of Marata is greatly reduced in numbers, but is still holding out and continues the war with the others. All of this lay beyond a second *despoblado,* to cross which required a passage of fifteen days.

Father Marcos may never have reached Cibola or Marata, and he said no more about the latter. As it turned out, his information was outdated perhaps by years. Meanwhile, Esteban and the advance party had arrived at Cibola, where the natives killed him and perhaps many of those with him. The survivors with Fray Marcos fled south all the way to Culiacan in the present Mexican state of Sinaloa. On September 2, 1539, the friar presented his report to the viceroy, devoid of any mentions of gold or treasure in the land of Cibola.

The viceroy, not entirely satisfied, dispatched Melchoir Diaz, Juan de Zaldivar, and a dozen horsemen on November 17, 1539, to verify the account of Father Marcos. Diaz and his companions rode north, probably to the beginning of the second *despoblado,* which could have placed them near the Gila River in modern-day southern Arizona. After halting in the vicinity of a site called *Chichilticale,* a Nahuatl word meaning "the red house," they spent the winter gathering information. In 1540 Coronado credited Fray Marcos with the introduction of this name, although it had not been included in his written report. Chichilticale was a pueblo ruin, probably of adobe, on or near the south side of the Gila River.

Diaz and Zaldivar were told that the people of Cibola ate salt from a lake two days' journey distant from Cibola, which could only be the Zuni Salt Lake in the Largo Creek drainage south of modern Fence Lake, New Mexico. They did not mention Marata by name but said, following their comments on Totonteac,

Also they tell me that there is a pueblo which is a single day's journey from Cibola and [that] they are at war with each other.

No one mentioned gold, but turquoises were abundant. All of this of course had come to them second-hand. Melchoir Diaz returned and reported to the viceroy on March 20, 1540.

Diaz had heard quite a lot about Cibola and the regions to the north, as we learn from a lengthy extract of his report included in an April 17, 1540 letter from Viceroy Mendoza to the King. Among other things,

It has been determined that Totonteac is seven short days' travel from the *provincia* of Cibola and that it is the same sort [of place], and the houses and people are also [the same]. And that there is cotton [there], [but] I doubt it since it is a cold land. [The informants] say that there are twelve *pueblos* [in Totonteac] [and] that each one is larger than the biggest one in Cibola.

In his early enthusiasm the previous October, Mendoza had already commissioned Francisco Vasquez de Coronado, governor of the province of Nueva Galacia, as leader of a large expedition to discover and take possession of the *reinos* and *provincias* of Marata, Acus, Cibola and the Seven Cities, and Totonteac. This small army included some 1300 Mexican Indians and at least

358 Spaniards who departed from Culiacan on April 22, 1540. By this time, Mendoza had read Diaz's discouraging report and he sought to recall the Coronado expedition, but it was too late. The Captain General and an advance guard were already on their way to Cibola. The rumored cities of gold lay ahead.

The surviving documents from Coronado's expedition have been translated and published several times and new ones may yet come to light. The army arrived at Cibola, now known as the Zuni Indian villages, in July 1540. They spent the next year and a half exploring the country east from there as far as central Kansas. With respect to their place names, historians are now generally agreed that Acus was the pueblo of Acoma while to the west lay Totonteac, a group of abandoned pueblos.

Before he reached the first *despoblado,* while still down in Mexico, Fray Marcos had started hearing about Totonteac. His informants there "examined [his] habit with their hands and told me that there was much of this [material] in Totonteac and that the natives of that place...wore clothes made of it." He laughed at that, and they replied:

Do you think that we do not know that what you wear and what we wear [are] different? You must understand that in Cibola all the houses are full of the clothing which we wear. But in Totonteac there are some small animals from which they remove [the fur], with which this [material] you are wearing is made.

The good father pursued this matter or, as he said, he sought to inquire in detail about the woolen cloth (his habit was of a gray, closely-woven woolen cloth):

And they told me that the animals are the size of [the] two Castilian greyhounds which Esteban had [with him]. They say that there are many [of them] in Totonteac. I could not ascertain what sort of animal it might be.

Perhaps Father Fray Marcos had just been introduced to the once-legendary antelope jackrabbit (*Lepus alleni*), specimens of which can reach twenty-one inches in length and thirteen pounds in weight; the largest hares in the western hemisphere.

In any event, when Father Marcos reached the populous area beyond this first *despoblado,* he:

...received another report about the woolen cloth of Totonteac. They say that the houses there are like those of Cibola, [though they are] better and much more numerous.

The elderly exile from Cibola whom he met subsequently expanded on this:

He also says that to the west is the *reino* they call Totonteac. He says that it is a [great] thing, the grandest in the world [with] the most people and the greatest wealth. Here [at Totonteac] they wear [the same] woolen cloth as what I wear is made from, as well as others even finer. [The fleeces] are obtained from the animals which they indicated to me farther back. They are a very civilized people and very different from the people whom I have seen [so far].

Later, as Fray Marcos was resting, as he says in sight of Cibola and contemplating whether to proceed or not, some of his native companions told him that in comparison with Cibola,

...that it [Cibola] was the least of the seven *ciudades* and that Totonteac is much grander and better than all the seven *ciudades*. And [they said] that Totonteac comprises so many buildings and people that it has no end. Considering the excellence of the *ciudad* it seemed [appropriate] to me to call that land the *Nuevo Reino de San Francisco.*

It was from Totonteac that the people of Cibola had secured their cotton. Those living at these now-abandoned pueblos had clothed themselves in rabbit-skin robes, probably the *paño* of Coronado. The Zuni Indians described that place to Coronado as now reduced to:

...a hot lake, around which are five or six dwellings (*case* in the Italian original). [They] also [say] that there used to be some others, but they have been destroyed during the wars.

Following the reasoning of archeologist Adolph Bandelier, Totonteac was probably the Homolovi group of ruins together with Chevelon pueblo and several others near present-day Winslow, Arizona. Although he did not attempt a visit, his inferences about it appear to be sound. Modern excavations there have yielded thousands of bones of cottontail and jack rabbits, and even a few of the *Lepus alleni* or antelope jackrabbit.

The Spanish captain Fernando de Alarcón, who had been sent by sea to resupply Coronado by sailing up the Colorado River, referred to a "river called Totonteac." This might well have been the Little Colorado. As for Fray Marcos' Marata, Coronado reported that "there is no *reino* of Marata here nor do the Indians have any information about it." Perhaps reading between the lines, the Zunis may have been telling him that it was none of his business, that Marata was no longer a problem. If he had known to ask using the names that the Zunis recognized in the late nineteenth century, i.e. Ma-Kia-tah and Kia'makia, their answer might have been very different.

For the next 350 years, no new references were made to the now-lost Kingdom of Marata. An emended version of Fray Marcos' report and several documents from the Coronado expedition appeared in Italian, Spanish, English, and finally in 1838 in French. No one showed the slightest interest in Marata, although the *reino* did make it onto at least two maps, in 1570 and 1657. The earlier one also showed Tototeac (*sic*).

Then in 1879–1880 ethnologists from the Smithsonian Institution descended on Zuni, initially Frank Hamilton Cushing and Matilda Coxe

Stevenson. Both lived at Zuni for a time, where they carried on extensive investigations and wrote at length about their findings. They focused on Zuni ceremonialism and had little interest in traditional history. The Zunis told Cushing that Marata was pronounced Ma-Kia-tah, and when he visited that site he found the ruins "both extensive and of remarkable construction." The archeologist Adolph Bandelier also came to Zuni and while he was aware of Marata from reading Fray Marcos' account, he relied upon Cushing's identification and did not visit the ruins.

We come down to two questions: Where was Marata located, and what led to its loss or destruction? Melchoir Diaz' account had placed it part-way between the Zuni pueblos and the Zuni Salt Lake, southeast of the former. An on-the-ground search by the author in 1994 determined that the only extensive pueblo ruin so situated bears the map name Fort Atarque. The origin of this name is not known. It does not lie on a trail from Hawikuh (a pueblo ruin west of Zuni Pueblo) to Acoma, as Cushing and Bandelier thought, but instead is adjacent to one of the trails that leads south from modern Zuni to the Zuni Salt Lake, as Stevenson said. She gave Kia'makia as the name of the ruin, whose inhabitants were the Kia'nakwe. Its walls still stood four to five feet high in 1884.

Cushing visited this site in 1880 and used the Zuni names Ma-tya-ta and Kia-ma-kia for the well-preserved ruins, which either he or an editor errored in placing along the wrong trail—one to Acoma instead of one to the Zuni Salt Lake. It is Stevenson's and Cushing's descriptions that confirm the identity of Kia'makia, Ma-tya-ta or Mak'yata as Marata.

Pottery at the site is very sparse but shows that the major pueblo was a very late prehistoric or protohistoric structure. The five-foot walls in 1884 are now reduced to two feet or less in height, due largely to disturbances by livestock. The general appearance and near-lack of pottery or other refuse, especially of any wood, suggest that the pueblo might still have been under construction when it was destroyed. Smaller pueblo ruins within the main enclosure are earlier in date and may have been razed in part for building material. The site area lies on both State of New Mexico and private lands, and visitors are not welcome.

Fray Marcos' informants indicated that the war between Cibola and Marata was ongoing, but Coronado learned in 1540 that the conflict had ended. Both Bandelier and Frederick Webb Hodge, also from the Smithsonian, noted that Spanish explorers were wont to pass along outdated information about places such as Marata and Totonteac. Hodge however wrote an intriguing paper that placed a chronological frame on the time when various clans joined to form the modern Navajo. He included the survivors of Marata as the Naqopà'-cine, forced from their old home near the salt lake, who joined the Navajo about 1536. While Hodge's arcane calculations are difficult or impossible to follow, the date of 1536 for the destruction of Marata would be an excellent match for the Spanish accounts.

Kia'makia was defeated by the Zunis following a four-day siege. Hodge inferred that the former inhabitants, now refugees, were "of Keresan stock," Keresan being a language group that also includes people of present-day Acoma, Zia, Santa Ana, Kewa (Santo Domingo) and Cochiti. There are a number of references to the Navajo clan he mentioned as the Nahoobáanii (horizontal gray streak people), Naxoba'ani and Nakhopani (brown streak horizontal on the ground). The geographical reference is to Santa Rita Mesa, a ridge line north of the Zuni Salt Lake.

While some of the Marata survivors perhaps became a clan of the early Navajos, Frank Cushing claimed that others, together with "parts of their ritual, strange[?] dances and language" were subsequently incorporated into the Zuni nation. Hodge had inferred as much, but it was Stevenson who described at length the quadrennial dance of the Kia'nakwe, who were clothed in white to represent ghost people angry with the Zunis for their destruction. The songs of the Kia'nakwe personators were "in the Sia tongue, which was the language of the Kia'nakwe." The dancers all belonged to the Corn clan. They were not really kachinas nor were they believed to live at the sacred lake. Thus in two modern Indian cultures do the Kia'nakwe survive today.

Other aspects are worth mentioning. Examination of the Kia'makia ruin shows that it has remarkable integrity, apart from minor excavations or vandalism by parties unknown. Around the perimeter, the distribution of stones from the original walls is almost entirely to the interior, which suggests that the exterior wall along the north side (180 meters in length) remained intact during the assault by the Zunis. A little south of the center of the west side, the wall was broken and stones scattered for some meters towards the interior. This may indicate the location where the Zunis created a breach, in their final assault at the end of the four-day siege.

What antagonism led to the war between the ancestral Zunis and the

Kia'nakwe? One answer may be that a trail from modern Zuni to their salt lake lies only 150 meters northwest of the ruin. Clearly, the establishment of this pueblo by other Indians presented a threat to the Zunis' access to their sacred salt lake. The Zunis' sentiments would probably have been analogous to those of Taos Pueblo to their Blue Lake. In the early sixteenth century, such a threat was met with violence.

The Zunis may also have been experiencing an economic problem. Aboriginally, the pueblos of Cibola acted as a funnel for the trade in *cueros de vaca*, bison hides. By 1539 this had become a huge affair; Fray Marcos estimated 2000 hides among the Sobaipuris alone. Yet it would have been a long distance, hundreds of miles, from Cibola to the bison plains in eastern New Mexico and western Texas. The bison may have been much closer. Excavations at Bat Cave on the southeastern edge of the Plains of San Augustine showed that this was a favorite camp of bison-hunters, as evidenced by the hundreds of bison bones and fragments of hides in the debris here. Campsites on the plains themselves have yielded more bison bones. Presumably the bison who once lived in this wide expanse of grassland were hunted out of existence.

Before that happened, bison may well have wandered even farther west. Along the north side of Jaralosa Wash, a broad valley immediately south of Kia'makia, an obvious bison petroglyph was included in a panel of rock art. One could argue that a group of intruders, Keresan-speakers from a group of pueblos that preceded Kia'makia, threatened a Zuni monopoly on access to a local source of bison hides. A relict population of even a few hundred bison would have been a resource not to be shared with interlopers. Between this and the threat regarding access to the Zuni Salt Lake, the Keresans had to go. By the time the metal men arrived, the situation had been resolved, and no one besides the talkative exile saw any reason to resurrect it.

2. Fray Marcos de Niza. Drawing by José Cisneros.

3. Marata on the Sanson Map of 1637. Sanson Map, 1637.

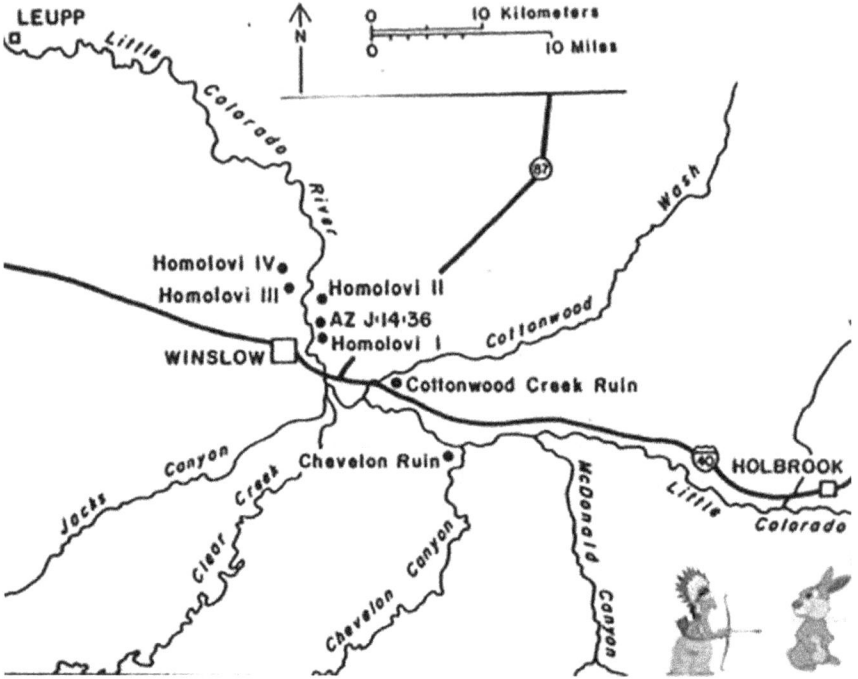

4. Ancient *reiño* of Totonteac. Map by the author.

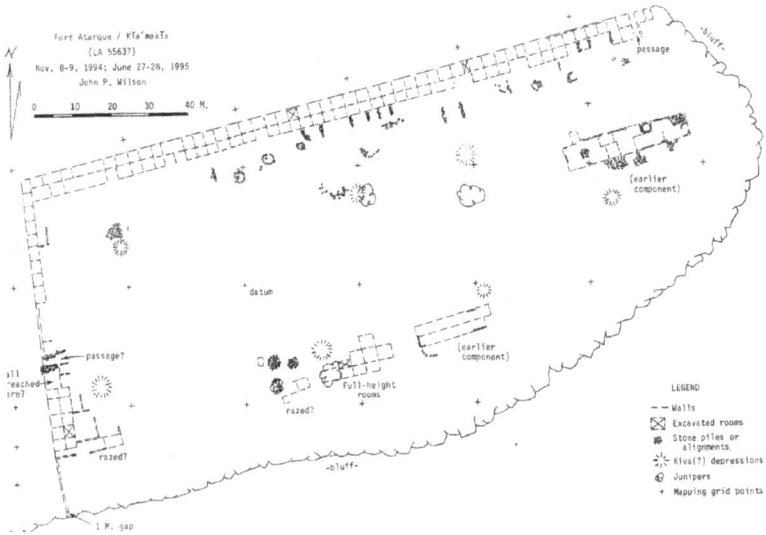

5. Kĭa'makĭa (Marata). Map by the author.

6. Section of the north wall, Kĭa'makĭa. Photograph by the author.

7. Kĭa'nakwe Gods dancing at Zuni. Photograph by Matilda Coxe Stevenson, 1904. Photo lot 23, Matilda Coxe Stevenson photographs, National Anthropological Archives, Smithsonian Institution.

8. Bison petroglyph along Jaralosa Draw. Photograph by the author.

REFERENCES

Adams, E. Charles, editor. 1996 *River of Change: Prehistory of the Middle Little Colorado River Valley, Arizona. Arizona State Museum, Archaeological Series 185.* Tucson.

Bandelier, A.F. 1890 Final Report of Investigations Among the Indians of the Southwestern United States, Carried on Mainly in the Years from 1880 to 1885. Part 1, esp. pp. 114, 120. Cambridge, Mass., John Wilson and Son.

————. 1890a Fray Marcos of Nizza. In *Contributions to the History of the Southwestern Portion of the United States,* Papers of the Archaeological Institute of America, Series V, pp. 106-178. Cambridge, Mass., John Wilson and Son.

————.1892 Final Report of Investigations Among the Indians of the Southwestern United States, Carried on Mainly in the Years from 1880 to 1885. Part II, esp. pp. 109, 327. Cambridge, Mass., John Wilson and Son.

————. 1892a An Outline of the Documentary History of the Zuni Tribe. In *A Journal of American Ethnology and Archaeology,* ed. by J. Walter Fewkes, Vol. III pp. 1-115. Cambridge, Mass., The Riverside Press. Note: The original manuscript including unpublished Chapters 4 and 5 is in the Peabody Museum at Harvard.

Baxter, Sylvester. 1881 Solved at Last. Mysteries of Ancient Aztec History Unveiled. Wonderful Achievements of Frank H. Cushing. In *Santa Fe Daily New Mexican,* June 23, 1881, p. 1.

Bunzel, Ruth L. 1932 Zuni Katcinas. In *47th Annual Report of the Bureau of American Ethnology, 1929–1930,* esp. pp.1009-1011. Washington, DC.

Craddock, Jerry R. 1999 Fray Marcos de Niza, *Relación* (1539): Edition and Commentary. In *Romance Philology* 53 Part 1 (Fall), pp. 69-118.

Cushing, Frank Hamilton. 1896 Outline of Zuni Creation Myths. In *Thirteenth Annual Report of the Bureau of American Ethnology, 1891–1892,* pp. 321-447. Washington, DC.

Dick, Herbert W. 1965 Bat Cave. School of American Research Monograph 27. Santa Fe, New Mexico.

Flint, Richard, and Shirley Cushing Flint, editors. 2005 Documents of the Coronado Expedition, 1539–1542. Dallas: Southern Methodist University Press.

Green, Jesse, editor. 1990 Cushing at Zuni. The Correspondence and Journals of Frank Hamilton Cushing 1879–1884. Albuquerque: University of New Mexico Press.

Hodge, Frederick Webb. 1895 "The Early Navajo and Apache." *American Anthropologist 8(O.S.),* pp. 223-240.

————. 1960 "Matyata." In *Handbook of American Indians North of Mexico, Part 1,* p.823. New York: Pageant Books Inc. Reprint of *Smithsonian Institution Bureau of American Ethnology Bulletin 30 Part 1* (1907). Also "Nakhopani" in same title *Part II,* p. 13.

Kelley, Klara. 1988 Archeological Investigations in West Central New Mexico, Volume 2: Historic Cultural Resources pp. 2-6 – 2-10. Bureau of Land Management, Las Cruces District, Socorro Resource Area.

Ladd, Edmund J. 1997 Zuni on the Day the Men in Metal Arrived. In *The Coronado Expedition to Tierra Nueva,* edited by Richard Flint and Shirley Cushing Flint, pp. 225-233. Niwot: University Press of Colorado.

Stevenson, Matilda Coxe. 1904 The Zuni Indians. In *Twenty-third Annual Report of the Bureau of American Ethnology, 1902–1902.* Washington, DC.

Van Valkenburgh, R.F. 1941 "Mesa Santa Rita" and "Marata." In *Diné Bikéyah,* pp, 92 and 94. Navajo Agency, U.S. Indian Service. Window Rock, Arizona.

Young, Robert W. and William Morgan, editors. 1954 The Different Navajo Clans. In *Navajo Historical Selections,* p. 21. Bureau of Indian Affairs, Phoenix Indian School Print Shop.

See also The Journey of Fray Marcos de Niza and The Mysterious Journey of Friar Marcos de Niza online. This chapter adapted from my website of the same name with supplemental material; to access the website enter: www.newmexico-civilwar and click on Marata in the links at the end. (This website is current as of the publication of this book.)

~ 2 ~

THE HOUSE OF FELIPE ROMERO

A SOURCE FOR NEW MEXICO SPANISH-COLONIAL HISTORY THAT LAWYERS of an earlier day were intimately familiar with, but which historians and anthropologists rarely ever consult, is the records of the U.S. Court of Private Land Claims, established in 1891. New Mexico became a territory in 1850, and the territorial office of Surveyor General was established in 1854. This official made recommendations to the U.S. Congress in regard to the land grants awarded under the laws of Spain and Mexico, from the late 17th century through the 1840s. At first, Congress routinely approved these, which meant that patents or land titles could be issued. By 1860, allegations of fraud held a cloud over the claims streaming in, and blanket approvals of New Mexico land titles stopped. In the absence of creditable documentation, Congress simply ceased to approve any more of the recommendations.

By 1890 the situation with clouded land titles had become impossible, since the most desirable lands for farming, ranching, and settlement were generally in areas covered by alleged land grants. None of the lands within the grants that Congress had not acted on could be given a clear title. The legislators in Washington finally dealt with this issue by creating the U.S. Court of Private Land Claims in 1891. The records of their proceedings in New Mexico are easily available on microfilm rolls at the University of New Mexico Library.[1] The actual records were once part of the General Land Office or Surveyor General's papers, which passed to the New Mexico office of the U. S. Bureau of Land Management, and currently are at the New Mexico State Records Center and Archives in Santa Fe.

Three kinds of questions were uppermost in the minds of the judges on the Court. Were the alleged land grants legitimate or were they frauds? If legitimate, were they community grants, issued to groups of prospective settlers, or were they private grants, awarded to individuals? Finally, what was the size of the grants and what were their boundaries? Many claims were not confirmed by the court, because (1) the claimants could not produce acceptable proof of their authenticity, (2) the authority named in the proffered documents lacked the legitimacy to issue such grants, or (3) the grantees did not fulfill the conditions set forth by the granting authority. Even when adjudged legitimate, the prospect of fraud existed if the extent or size of the claims appeared to have been inflated. The identification of boundary calls could be a major problem, as these were universally given with reference to natural landmarks, traditional place names, and the boundaries of contiguous grants made at earlier dates. Size was occasionally a factor; many of the Pueblo Indian land grants were limited to four square leagues.

The files shown in the microfilms are incomplete; some transcripts have omissions, appeals are not included, and court decisions may be absent. All of these parts can be found elsewhere. In my own experience in browsing the films, it appeared that many of the testimonies were concerned with land grant boundaries. The reader will find precious little, if anything, about what lay within the boundaries, even if whole villages already existed inside the borders.

The case that intrigued me most was the Sevilleta Land Grant, which lay to either side of the Rio Grande about forty miles south of Albuquerque, between there and Socorro.[2] Named for a Piro Indian pueblo situated on a bluff along the east side of the Rio Grande, Sevilleta or "Little Seville" was abandoned at the time of the Pueblo Revolt in 1680 when most of the Pueblo Indians drove the Spaniards out of New Mexico. The inhabitants at Sevilleta left with the refugees. Although the Spaniards returned to New Mexico in 1693, the lands below Belen remained unoccupied until 1800. In that year the Governor of New Mexico, Fernando Chacón, was ordered to resettle four communities, these being the locations of Piro Indian pueblos in the 17th century.[3] The governor acted at the behest of the Comandante General in Chihuahua and reported back to him that it simply wasn't possible to resettle all four at once, but he would start with two—Alamillo, and a few months later, Sevilleta.

The initial effort did not go well. We have a detailed account of what happened in the case of the attempted resettlement of Alamillo. In a letter of March 31, 1800, the governor reported to the Comandante General in Chihuahua that:

"The said new settlement [Alamillo] consists up to this present time, of sixty-two families, for the gathering of whom I published a proclamation through all the province, in order that all the poor people having no lands or means of working them, would voluntarily enlist themselves; but this notice having had no effect, it was necessary to use force and take hold of the day laborers, servants, gamblers, those living in concubinage, and the incorrigibles in going without permission to the heathens. As a result of the departure of these people some commotion was noticed in various jurisdictions and particularly in the Capital, wherefore it was necessary to send the troops to aid the judges."[4]

We are told little about what happened a few months later, when the resettlement at Sevilleta was undertaken:

"The settlers of the aforesaid place of Servilleta (sic) settled in a fortification in the form of a square, with all possible security and they immediately began a plaza of stone and adobes, which, it is possible, may not be finished this year, on account of its great proportions."[5]

The lands surrounding the ruined pueblo of Sevilleta were permanently resettled by sixty-seven New Mexican families. A generation later in May of 1819, attorney Carlos Galvadon petitioned the nearest authority, the Alcalde of Belen (the Belen Land Grant dated from 1740) for lands designated for use of the people at Sevilleta. The alcalde forwarded the petition to Governor Facundo Melgares, who approved it and directed it back to him to assign the usual land to the petitioners and to prepare title documents.

On June 4, 1819, the alcalde placed the inhabitants of Sevilleta in possession of a tract of land he described as being bounded...

On the north by the boundary of Sabinal; on the south by the Alamillo Arroyo, on the opposite side of the Arroyo called the San Lorenzo Creek; on the east by a mountain in front of said town; and on the west by the Ladrones Mountains.[6]

The grant document then became part of the Archives of New Mexico.

The inhabitants of Sevilleta continued in uncontested possession of their lands, a private land grant, until October 1874 when attorney Samuel Ellison filed a petition asking the Surveyor General to confirm the grant. The Surveyor General investigated and found that the muniments of title were genuine and beyond question. He recommended that Congress confirm the claim to the sixty-seven original grantees or their heirs and representatives. Congress took no action. A preliminary survey made in March and April, 1878, by deputy surveyors Sawyers and White, showed that the lands covered some 224,770.13 acres on both sides of the Rio Grande.[7]

Then in December 1892 two descendants of the original grantees filed suit in the Court of Private Land Claims, praying for confirmation of the grant to themselves and other heirs and assigns of the original grantees. The United States was not able to advance any defense against recognition of the claim, and one year later the court confirmed the Sevilleta Land Grant to the heirs of the original grantees. The court's decree on December 4, 1893, defined the boundaries as follows:

"...on the north, the boundary of Sabinal, being a portion of the grant to Belen, and more particularly designed by the ruins of the hacienda of Felipe Romero and the point of the Sabinal hill (*la punta de la loma de Sabinal*) lying due east and west of each other;..."[8]

Therein a problem arose, for while the language in the grant clearly allowed for some flexibility in assigning boundaries on the ground, it was the north boundary that proved to be the greatest problem. In the spring of 1895, Deputy U.S. Surveyor Albert Easley ran the north boundary as a due east and west line passing over the highest point of Sabinal hill and what were pointed out to him as the ruins of (the house of) Felipe Romero. The latter were almost completely obliterated. Later that same year, the U.S, Attorney filed his objections to Easley's survey as not confirming to the boundary calls of the court's decree. Amended objections were made in 1897. Meanwhile the case had been reopened in 1896 following a protest by representatives of the Belen grant, who also objected to approval of the Easley survey. The Belen objections were that this survey located the north boundary of the Sevilleta Grant about two miles north of the southern boundary of the Belen Grant, which preceded it in time.[9]

At the new hearing (1896) Easley testified as to how he determined his boundary calls on the north, and his uncertainty about the reliability of the identification of Felipe Romero's house. The protestors asked for a new survey, and the proceedings were labeled Felipe Peralta and Tomás Cordoba, Commissioners, vs. United States.[10] The hearings run to some seventy pages, the principal subject being the interrogation of local residents on the locations of boundary calls, particularly for the north boundary. The government presented a total of eight witnesses. The consensus among them was that indeed the north boundary of the grant west of the Rio Grande was an old monument at the point of the Sabinal hill; and to the east side of the river it was the ruins of the house of Felipe Romero. These, as noted above, were said to lie east and west of one another. Six of the witnesses who testified placed the ruins of Felipe's house between one and one-and-one-half miles north of the mouth of the Arroyo Tio Maes.

The time was now 1897 and the interviews became more interesting as they moved from witness to witness. Cross-examinations were done by a well-known New Mexico attorney who often represented land grant claimants—Thomas B. Catron. Much of his questioning was taken up with establishing the nature of this north boundary east of the river; that is, with the ruins of the house of Felipe Romero. Catron asked what was the source of the witnesses' information? Most of them had seen the ruins, at various times, and they claimed that their attribution of the ownership came from their grandfathers, or that it was common knowledge. No one had ever known Felipe Romero; no one had ever known anyone to live at his house during their lifetimes.

It soon became evident that the witnesses were relying to some extent upon one man, Jesus Baca Y Garcia, ninety-one years old, who had shown them the ruins and said that this was where Felipe Romero had lived before the Sevilleta Grant was given, but that he had been driven out by Apaches and went back to Belen. Baca was the only one who said that his *grandfather* had seen Felipe Romero living in this house. The consensus from the testimony was that nobody had ever actually seen the man (Romero) and that the house had been in ruins as long as anybody could remember.

Catron recognized that the identification of these ruins, and hence the north boundary of the grant along the eastern side of the Rio Grande, might hinge upon the testimony of Jesus Baca y Garcia. Baca had taken a special agent of the court and several of the other witnesses to the site on March 10, 1897. Through his lengthy cross-examination, Catron "established" that the ruins as of 1897 were only five yards or more east of the eastern bank of the river, more than ten yards out from the western edge of the hills, and that the acequia of La Joya intervened between the ruins and the river. When Baca was fifteen, the ruined house had been about 200 yards east of the river.

In the course of his questioning of Mr. Baca and several of the other witnesses, Catron brought out an incredible number of details about the nature of the house. It was claimed to be a little ranch of which two rooms, very small, remained. These had stone foundations, made of uncut stone. The stones were almost at the surface; loose but not much scattered. A doorway opened towards the south. One witness thought the walls had been made of turf blocks cut from the adjacent meadow; the others implied that these were adobe and had stood about a yard high as of 1820, but had been reduced to the foundations by 1890. A fireplace, indicated by some burned adobe, lay in the room to the east, in one of the north corners. The questions and replies went 'round and 'round upon these and related points, through many pages of testimony Occasionally the process became frustrating for the witnesses, as when Catron established (with Baca) that there were no remains of additional rooms and only one fireplace, in the east room:

"Q. – Was that where the kitchen was?

"A. – I was not the cook."

Sometimes irrelevancies crept in, one of which indicated that the witness (Baca again) and the attorney had a long prior acquaintance. The witness' grandfather was a settler at Sabinal who died when Baca was about thirty. At that time Baca's daughter was more than twenty years of age:

"A. (witness) – "…you know everything about my business; my daughter made the bed for you."

Perhaps he gave more information than anyone really needed to know.

After reading through this material, one becomes curious as to who Felipe Romero was anyway and why had this ruined house of his become such a focus of the testimony? One can look in the papers for the adjoining grant to the north, the Belen Land Grant, and learn that one boundary call was given as:

"…on the south, the place called Phelipe Romero (believed near Sabinal)…."

The Belen grant was given in November 1740. If this was the case, the implication is that the site was in ruins in 1740. If so, it's little wonder that nobody ever knew Felipe Romero or anyone else living at the house.[11]

To check further on this, one can look into the itineraries of travelers who followed the Camino Real up and down the Rio Grande. Nicolas de la Fora's description from August 14, 1766, had him traversing the four leagues from the ruins of Sevilleta pueblo to the next community to the north (Las Nutrias), in the course of which…

"About halfway along this road are the ruins of the houses of Felipe Romero."[12]

When Bishop Tamarón visited New Mexico in 1760, he went up and back along the river and passed the ruins of Felipe Romero's estancia. His journal entry for May 18, 1760 stated that in the middle of that day they came to the site of Sevilleta pueblo…

"....and a little beyond it the ruined estancia of Felipe Romero. Both were lost with the kingdom."[13]

Another traveler, Brigadier Pedro de Rivera, passed the ruins of numerous farmsteads and haciendas north of Socorro when he entered New Mexico in 1726. His journal entries for May 30-31 mentioned spacious meadows and vast woodlands to either side of the river here, but he made no references to named sites between the ruined pueblo of Sevilleta and the *paraje* of Las Nutrias some eight leagues beyond.[14]

On the strength of the clue offered by Bishop Tamarón, the next step was to jump back to the records of the Pueblo Revolt and the Reconquest, to see if the witnesses who gave testimony in the 1890s might have been talking about something that was really old. Sure enough, when you look at Governor Diego de Vargas' journals for the period of the reconquest, 1692–1693, what did the Spaniards see when they followed up the river? They passed the rancho of Felipe Romero, abandoned at an earlier time, or as Vargas said in his journal entry for September 4, 1692:

"I, the governor and captain general, arrived with the camp at this abandoned pueblo of Sevilleta. To provide for the horses and mules, I went on ahead to the estancia they say belonged to Felipe Romero. I called a halt there since the site had abundant pasture."[15]

What the witnesses were really talking about was a pre-Rebellion rancho, and they were correctly attributing it to its original owner more than 200 years after he had lived there.

We know a little more about the man. Captain Felipe Romero was a native of New Mexico born about 1639. He married Jacinta de Guadalajara y Quirós. He and Bartolomé Gómez Robledo were accused of killing cattle belonging to Alamillo Pueblo in 1661, Alamillo being another Piro pueblo located a few leagues south of Sevilleta, between there and Socorro. This implies that Felipe, with his wife and eventually six sons and four daughters, lived at their pre-Rebellion rancho twenty years before the Pueblo Revolt. They escaped at the time and presumably went south in company with other refugees from the Sandia and Socorro areas. In El Paso, Romero enlisted as a soldier before Governor Otermín and probably participated in Otermín's attempted reconquest, after which he showed up in documents, signing petitions and whatnot, in the El Paso area as late as 1684. He and his wife were reportedly deceased by 1695, although one of the *noticias* (from 1776) of Juan Candelaria, born in 1692, said that the house of Felipe Romero (perhaps a son?) stood at the Cañada de Juan Lopez, less than four leagues southwest of Santa Fe.[16]

To return to the case involving the ruined house, and particularly its location, the proceedings became very tangled as additional witnesses, especially those for the grantees, were introduced. Catron proceeded to demolish the creditability of Jesus Baca y Garcia by calling up witnesses of his own and recalling some of the government witnesses. The first such person, a witness for the grantees, was Tomás Cordova, who supervised a ditch repair project in 1867. Through questioning him and others, Catron established that the location given earlier by Baca was where men from La Joya had camped for between a week and a month while repairing an irrigation ditch. They left campfires through this area, brought in stones, and also left one or more piles of stones, the latter having been covered by sand as of 1897. This was just north of the mouth of the Arroyo Tio Maes. Catron's own witnesses and two of the recalled government witnesses consistently placed the house of Felipe Romero from one to one-and-one-half miles *north* of the Arroyo Tio Maes. They also knew of no ruins between the two places or of any ruins in the valley of the Arroyo Tio Maes prior to their camp.

The court in its September 1897 decision found that the north boundary of the Sevilleta Grant had been erroneously described in its December 4, 1893 decree, which led to the Easley survey. It modified the previous degree by ordering a resurvey that moved the north boundary line about a mile south of the first line. The Sevilleta and Belen grants still overlapped and in consequence of the Belen grant being the earlier one and having priority, another resurvey was ordered and a patent issued to the owners of the Sevilleta Land Grant based on the description in the revised field notes on February 8, 1907. The dividing line between the two grants then became what is shown on the present USGS Abeytas7.5' quadrangle map as the Belen Grant South Boundary, which very nearly coincides with the mouth of the [Tio] Maes Arroyo.

At the end, the location of the ruins of the house of Felipe Romero became irrelevant. In the first round of questioning in 1897, no one had queried the grantee's claim for the actual location of the house. This writer sought to find it in 1971 and again in 1975, and did locate a small patch of orange-colored adobe and some mounding along the roadway that parallels the east side of the La Joya Ditch, about where the indicated Casa Colorado South Boundary line on the USGS map intersects the ditch.[17] No artifacts or traces of adobe bricks were seen. The location is about one-and-one-quarter miles north from the mouth of Arroyo Tio Maes.

The evidence brought out during the hearings showed that the remains seen by surveyor Easley were actually the ruins of the house of Jesus Baca, presumably not the same person as one of the witnesses. In any event, the details that attorney Catron pursued with such diligence had no real bearing on the resolution of the case.

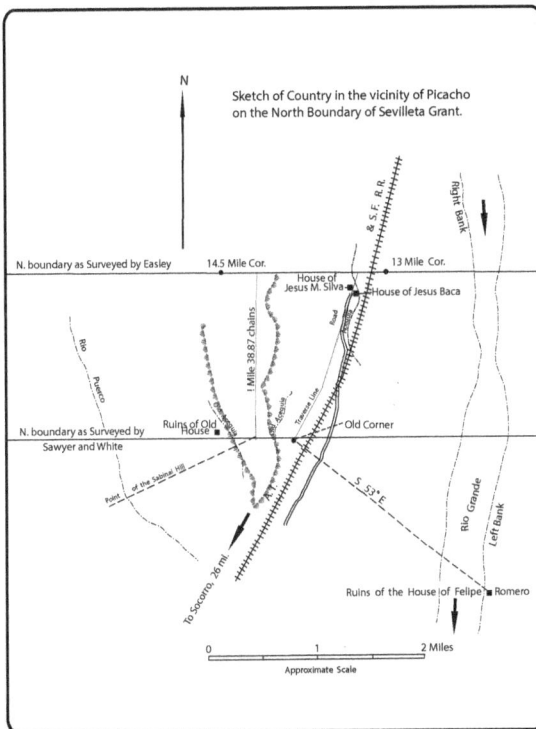

N

Sketch of Country in the vicinity of Picacho
on the North Boundary of Sevilleta Grant.

9. North boundary of Sevilleta Grant, with the house
of Felipe Romero. Map by the author.

NOTES

1. See Land records of New Mexico, microfilm F799.L36 1955 at Zimmerman Library CSWR, University of New Mexico. A 1987 refilming of these documents is also available.

2. Land records of New Mexico, Case #55, Microfilm Reel 38.

3. Ralph Emerson Twitchell, *The Spanish Archives of New Mexico, Vol.* 1, p. 358 document #1199; Pedro de Nava to the Governor of New Mexico, 11 June 1800.

4. Chacon to Pedro de Nava, 31 March, 1800. In Twitchell, op. cit., p. 345 document #1155.

5. Chacon to Pedro de Nava, 5 July, 1800. In Twitchell, op.cit., p. 370 document #1266. English translations of this and the foregoing documents are among the WPA records at the Fray Angélico Chávez Library in Santa Fe, New Mexico, also on microfilm as WPA translations of Spanish Archives of New Mexico I, CSWR microfilm CD 3394 T722 1999.

6. J.J. Bowden, *Private Land Claims in the Southwest,* Vol. 2. Master of Laws in Oil and Gas thesis, Southern Methodist University (1969), pp. 190-191.

7. Bowden, pp. 191-192.

8. Bowden, p. 192.

9. Bowden, pp. 192-193; also Land records of New Mexico Case #55, Microfilm Reel 38.

10. Bowden, pp. 192-194; also Land records of New Mexico Case #55 Microfilm Reel 38.

11. Gilberto Espinosa and Tibo J. Chaves, *El Rio Abajo* (Pampa, Texas, n.d.), p. 76.

12. Lawrence Kinnaird, *The Frontiers of New Spain.* The Quivira Society, Berkeley (1958 reprint), p. 89.

13. Eleanor B. Adams, ed, "Bishop Tamaron's Visitation of New Mexico, 1760," *New Mexico Historical Review* 28(3) (1953), p. 201.

14. Brigadier Pedro de Rivera, *Diario y Derrotero* . México, Archivo Historico Militar Mexicano, Núm 2 (1946), pp. 50-51.

15. John L. Kessell and Rick Hendricks, eds., *By Force of Arms* (1992), p. 375.

16. "Information Communicated by Juan Candelaria Resident of this Villa de San Francisco Xavier de Albuquerque Born 1692 – Age 84." *New Mexico Historical Review* 4(3): 284.

17. U.S. Geological Survey Abeytas 7.5' Quad Map (1952).

3

REPORT OF A SCOUT BY CAPTAIN THOMAS CLAIBORNE

REGIMENT OF MOUNTED RIFLEMEN [R.M.R.], 1860.

FROM THE TIME OF ITS ORIGINAL SETTLEMENT, THE PROVINCE AND LATER THE territory of New Mexico had been in contention with the surrounding Apache and Navajo Indians. The United States inherited this problem after 1846 and stationed soldiers at various locations to offer protection to the citizens and hopefully maintain the appearance of peace.

One group of raiders was the Mescalero Apaches, who lived principally in the Sacramento Mountains of south-central New Mexico and beyond into far western Texas. There were no civilian settlements east of the Río Grande Valley and south of the upper Pecos River country, and it was to the farms and villages in these areas that the Mescaleros directed their raiding for livestock and other plunder.

The Army made a number of ineffectual forays into the Mescalero country from 1849 on, and by 1854 one commander determined to make war on the Apaches after they ignored his naive order that they cease raiding. This did not go well. On January 19, 1855, Captain Henry Stanton led a party of his 1st Dragoons into an ambush near the Río Peñasco on the east side of the Sacramentos, which resulted in his own death and that of two private soldiers. The other troops wisely withdrew. The death of a captain in combat was viewed as a major setback, and the department commander answered this by establishing a new post in the Mescalero country, naming it Fort Stanton.

Among the Mescalero leaders, cooler heads prevailed and they requested a conference with the New Mexico governor, David Meriwether, which led to a peace treaty concluded in May 1855. Although the treaty was never ratified by Congress, the Indians generally abided by it and an uneasy peace settled over eastern New Mexico and the Sacramento Mountains country.

Settlers flocked to the valleys of the Río Bonito and the Río Ruidoso beginning in 1855, feeling assured of protection by the Army. This created new problems, as the Fort Stanton commanders then had to contend with the newcomers selling whiskey to the Indians, which encouraged them to raid the civilians' livestock.

Farms and small ranches along the Río Bonito were largely inhabited by Hispanic setters, while their counterparts in the valley of the Río Ruidoso seem to have been Anglo-Americans. One exception was Washington Peck, whose stone house apparently survives as a small ruin actually within the right-of-way of highway US 380 above Hondo, New Mexico. Peck wisely sold out in 1861 and relocated in Oregon. In recent years, one of his descendants returned and found the tumbled remains of Peck's house now claimed by a large rattlesnake!

As late as 1860, New Mexico south of the Río Ruidoso was still unknown and completely unsettled except by the native Mescalero Apache Indians. A view of this land in its original state and a rough map were given in the report of another Army captain, Thomas Claiborne, whose company from the Regiment of Mounted Riflemen traversed it in late January 1860, responding to the theft of horses from Mr. Peck's *rancho*. Captain Claiborne's mission was a peaceful one, and his report has enduring value in offering an account of the lofty ridges and desolate plains seen there, as well as the native Apaches. His punctuation and grammar have been improved as necessary.

Fort Stanton N.M. Jany. 31st 1860

Sir

I have the honor to report in writing the results of the scout ordered from your office on [the] 24th inst.

The command consisted of 4 Sergts., 2 Corpls., 39 pvts. of B Co. & 1 Bugler, 2 Corporals, 12 pvts. of D Co. R.M.R., the Hospital Steward Noisane and one Captain. The object [was] the pursuit of a party of Apaches who had taken some 8 or 10 head of horses from settlers below this Post on the Bonita River. Owing to the lateness of the session of the Genl. C. Martial of which I was a member on the 24th, I did not get farther that night than Capt. Hare's house 13 miles below here. About 8 o'clock 25th inst. I joined the command, which under Lieutenant R. Jones had preceded me to the junction of the rivers at Mr. Peck's place. Here I was joined by Mr. Peck Jr. & Mr. Wood. The morning was very stormy & the snow fell fast 'till about 9 o'clock A.M.

When the clouds broke away, the way by which the trail led was up a cañon southerly & southwesterly to a large lake. I kept straight on to the Pajarito Camp, which lies about 25 miles due south of this post. A good camp of grass & a grove of fine oaks, cedar & pine was got on the southeast side. The water is brackish. Early on 26th [with] the guides Chatto & Mariano, Indians, leading I set off south, the old Indian trail being followed along the feet of the ridges, bending to the southeast to avoid the high ridges.

At about 15 miles watered at a spring & again struck the trail of the stolen animals. The trail here goes over a very high ridge, thence down a narrow cañon winding four or five miles S. westerly 'till it emerges on a high rolling plain surrounded by the lofty ridges which break off to the east from the Sacramento Mts. [At] 12 miles struck the Peñasco River, a bold & clear stream coming from the west from high ridges on which were seen patches of snow & ice. I have at about 2½ o'c P.M. struck a fresh trail which came down the river & led along the left bank. I followed it 'till near sundown & camped 6 or 8 miles below where I first struck the river. Early the next morning 27th [I] set off on the trail & in one hour & a half came upon a camp of four men with several women & children, which proved to be that of Josecíto. Two men & two or three women & children waited our approach; the others in camp took to the thick willows which here bound the river.

On finding that the party had to all appearances nothing whatever to do with the robbery, I proceeded onward to the camp of Negrito, which I reached in four hours, crossing a large bend of the Peñasco. I expected to get information from him; he expressed much concern at seeing the troops & offered to go with us & look for Ojo Blanco & his son, who were the real thieves. He thought that as they were guilty, they would hide in the most difficult places, but if he could find the trail he could & would follow it. I told him he must go with us. He also told me that Enero Viejo was only a short distance off, & that Mancos' band were hunting antelope in the direction of the Pecos. That he & they were friendly & desired to be & would do all in their power to take the son of Ojo Blanco & deliver him up. This I impressed upon him as very necessary & that on coming to the Fort the man must be produced, but that he must go with me now & try to find him.

Accordingly, next morning I set off on the return up the Peñasco & camped where I first struck it, at which place the tracks of the stolen animals were lost. Before I got to the camp, I saw two Indians on horseback and, taking the 1st section, galloped up to them. They quietly waited my coming & proved to be men of Dalgo's camp. The latter presently came over the hill. They were out hunting & their camp was several miles west; [they] told me they were friendly & were determined to be so as they wished to pass about unmolested, Dalgo commenting that he had a "good head" and was "no fool," had not seen Ojo Blanco & did not know where his camp was, had seen the trail of shod horses while hunting & that it led back towards the Bonita. This was true as regards the trail of the shod horses, all of which, four in number, had escaped from the Indians & returned to Mr. Peck's place.

Two unshod horses were still missing, the tracks of which were not to be distinguished from those of the many Indians' horse tracks thereabouts. On [the] 28th, I tried to induce the guides to lead me into the hills which lay between the trail by which I had come down to the Peñasco & this main ridge which is the Sacramento Mts. As I had previously understood them to say, there were three water holes in there & I judged this party of Ojo Blanco to be hid in those hills, but they only evinced there was no Apache in that direction & to all propositions, they only said he might be in one place or another of many hiding places in the Mts. I suggested then Dog Cañon. They said no Indians were there now & it was five days' travel. After looking for any tracks that could lead me further on, the Indians gave it up, Negrito saying that he would now go back to his camp & in eight days come to the Fort & promised to seize on Ojo Blanco's son whenever & wherever he could find him. I gave up this chase as hopeless & returned to the Pajarito Camp of the 25th. I [on the] next day marched directly North for this Post, arriving here yesterday, having lost no animals but all somewhat jaded. I found the grass tolerably good. The weather was cold, at times severe, & again quite pleasant.

I observed in the trail leading hence to the Pajarito a single horse track which I believe was the trail of a courier to Ojo Blanco from the Indians near here. I saw Enero Viejo; I do not believe that any of the Indians had anything to do with the robbery as Ojo Blanco's son is the guilty one. There is a river I believe not heretofore known [Río Felix], 16 miles north of the Peñasco, quite as large for the distance it runs as the Peñasco. I watered my horses at a spring which issues from the [bed] at that place, dry bed of the river for it sinks and rises & is alternately lost in the plain towards the Pecos. Its direction is southeasterly as is the general lay of the ridges. There is a vast deal of cedar, a good deal of pine & occasionally scrub oaks in the valleys and gorges of the hills. All the valleys are of a rich black mould & many of the hills & ridges are of a rich soil when it has not been washed away & left the bare fragments of limestone, which is found to be the strata of all the hills; saw a little granite at the Pajarito Mt.

The appearance of the country low down on the Peñasco is very desolate. The Mts. on the left bank are bare & the plains [are] covered with fragments of limestone, with patches of good grass in the valleys but a few miles inward to the Mts. on the right bank to a point 14 miles below where I struck it. The guides said there was much trees but on the immediate bank of the river nothing but a chain of lofty bald knobs is visible; a very few cottonwoods on the river. But I saw canes 12 or 14 feet high in very extensive & very rich bottoms of several thousand acres extent in one place. Below the point above mentioned is a most dreary perspective of desolate & unwatered plains & a long range of bald hills to the west. A faint blue line in the far south marked the place of the Guadalupe Mts.

I heard after I left Josecíto's camp that a brother of Berancio's who for a year past has lived with that band, in his fear threw himself into the river to cross it & was drowned. I saw where his body was found on my return by the camp. I again have occasion & I state with pleasure that I consider Hospital Steward Edmund Noisane as every way worthy of confidence & the respect of all officers, always cheerful & respectful & ready for the performance of his duties. The whole command behaved admirably & were eager for an affair. I was only sorry that after every effort it was denied to us. I could have destroyed the four camps I surprised easily, but I was after the guilty alone. The scout has had a very wholesome effect, I believe, if I may judge of the conduct & appearance of those I saw.

Very Respectfully,

Yr. Obt. St.,
Th. Claiborne, Capt. R.M.R.
Lieutenant R. Jones R.M.R.
Cmg. Scout

Lt. R. Jones R.M.R.
Adjt. Gen.

[Sketch of the lay of the Country:]

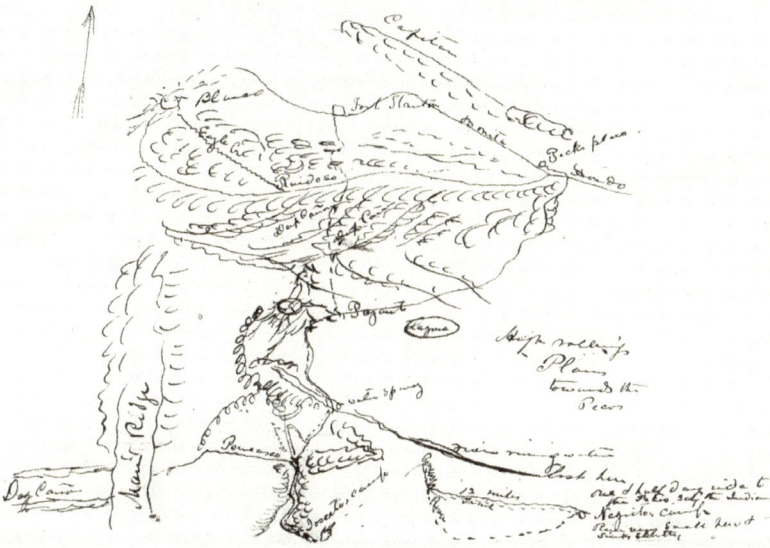

10. Captain Claiborne's Map of the Sacramento Mountains country, 1860.
U.S. National Archives and Records Service.

11. Rio Peñasco in the Winter.
Scott Land Company, Dimmitt,
Texas.

12. Apache Indian Camp. University of Arizona Special Collections Library.

REFERENCES

Brooks, Clinton E., and Frank D. Reeve, editors. 1947 James A. Bennett: A Dragoon in New Mexico, 1850–1856. New Mexico Historical Review 22(1) pp. 51-97; 22(2) pp. 140-176. The first installment is followed by 5 pp. of transcribed documents regarding the Mescaleros in the fall of 1855.

Kiser, William S. 2012 Dragoons in Apacheland. Norman: University of Oklahoma Press.

Myers, Lee. 1993 Fort Stanton, New Mexico: The Military Years 1855–1896. Lincoln County Historical Society Publication No. 2.

Ryan, John P. 1988 Fort Stanton and Its Community 1855–1896. Las Cruces: Yucca Tree Press.

U.S. National Archives, Microcopy M-1120 Roll 11, File No. C-2.

4

DELIVERING THE MAIL, LONG, LONG AGO

BEFORE YOU COMPLAIN TOO MUCH ABOUT THE COST AND DELAYS IN POSTAL service, consider what people used to go through. In 1851 it cost only 3¢ per half-ounce to send a letter up to 3,000 miles. Twelve years later, the same 3¢ would carry this letter anywhere in the United States. While first-class letter rates have increased eighteen-fold since then, a recent experience confirmed that delivery times may be no better now than during the Civil War.

Another change besides the increased cost is that private contractors once carried the mail between post offices, over thousands of designated postal routes. Having the right political connections usually counted more than submitting the low bid in winning such a contract. For shorter routes a buggy or 'mail hack' might be used, while on longer runs such as Route No. 8076 between San Antonio and El Paso, Texas, stagecoaches conveyed both passengers and mail over the 700-mile distance. On the longest single run, coaches departing San Francisco on the 2,800 mile drive to St. Louis, Missouri, might carry up to 10,000 letters at 10¢ each, in addition to passengers and their luggage. In the east, some of the railroad trains included mail cars.

Getting your letter to the post office was just part of the process. Stamp collectors who specialize in complete envelopes, called covers, are aware that 19th century examples may bear only the name, the city or post office, and state of the recipient, such as Mrs. Louisa M. Roe, Adams, Adams County, Illinois. This would probably be returned for insufficient address today, but in great-great-grandmother's time, before home delivery and P.O. boxes, people expecting mail had to ask for it at their local post office. Today we call this General Delivery. Newspapers occasionally published long lists of the names of persons for whom letters were waiting. The first home deliveries of mail began in New York City and forty-eight other larger cities in 1863. Now an address required a street name and house or apartment number.

If a postmaster had enough office space, he or she might ease the unavoidable crowding and jostling of everyone demanding their mail at once by opening separate delivery windows for ladies and gentlemen. Even so, a young bride like Louisa Roe might have found a visit to the post office unsetting, if the following anecdote found in an 1864 Quincy, Illinois newspaper indeed happened. A carefully staged diversion, as we see, could resolve the problem entirely:

"The girls who crowd through a file of men to get their letters in the Post Office must read this:

'Oh, dear,' exclaimed Mary, throwing herself into the rocking chair. 'I'll never go to the Post Office again, to be looked out of countenance by all those men standing around the halls and near the ladies' delivery. It's so provoking! What can I do, Minerva, to stop those awful men from staring me in the face?'

'Do as I do,' replied Minerva, with a sly look, 'show them your ankles.'"

Postoffice Notice.

ARRIVAL OF MAILS.

FROM THE EAST. From **Santa Fé,** on Mondays, Wednesdays, and Fridays, at 12 o'clock at night.

FROM THE SOUTH. From **El Paso,** Texas, on Mondays, Thursdays, and Saturdays. **POSTOFFICE HOURS. No deviation from this Rule.** Every day, from 7 to 9 o'clock A.M., and from 4 to 6 o'clock P.M.; and on the arrival of mails, one hour thereafter.

POSTOFFICE, *New Building, Main Street, Albuquerque, N.M.*

MELCHIOR WERNER, Postmaster.

13. Post Office notice, 1867. *The Albuquerque Press,* February 16, 1867.

REFERENCES

Quincy (Illinois) *DailyWhig and Republican,* May 30, 1864, page 2.

Various issues of the San Francisco *Daily Alta California* 1859-1861, reporting the numbers of letters carried by Butterfield Overland Mail stages departing for the east.

"Report of the Postmaster General" October 31, 1863, in 38th Cong 1st Sess., House Exec. Doc. 1 (1864), Serial Set #1184.

Websites listing postage rates through the years.

$$\sim 5 \sim$$

MURDER MOST FOUL: PINOS ALTOS IN 1860

PINOS ALTOS, OR PINO ALTO AS IT WAS KNOWN THEN, GREW RAPIDLY INTO A boomtown after the initial discovery of placer gold along Bear Creek in mid-May of 1860. Miners flocked into this foothill country about ten miles west of the Santa Rita copper mines in southwestern New Mexico. Newspapers from Texas to California carried excited reports by volunteer correspondents. In August of that year the census recorded five hundred persons at the Pino Alto Gold Mines.[1] Although people continuously came and went, this was in quite a contrast with newspaper claims that thousands of people were on their way to the mines and that the Mexican and American populations were approximately equal in numbers.[2] About 90% of the miners gave Mexico or New Mexico as their place of birth.

Actual descriptions of Pino Alto at this time are scarce. One, written by a lawyer from Virginia named Benjamin Neal, said that the two-month-old town had some eight or ten stores besides grog shops and gambling houses. Almost in spite of the abundance of whiskey, gambling halls and well-armed men, together with some ethnic tension, Pino Alto was not a disorderly camp. Attorney Neal claimed that "Each mining district has its own laws, and it is astonishing how the people quietly and peaceably obey them."[3] James Tevis, who also lived there at this time, recalled in later years that Sundays were used for dueling and all difficulties were settled on that day, provided the contending parties were sober.[4] An early issue of the nearest newspaper, *The Mesilla Times,* carried an account of one such duel between Henry Kennedy and "Sam" Dyer. Dyer received a slight scratch on his knuckles; Kennedy was unhurt.[5]

Although any current map will show Pinos Altos well within New

Mexico and a few miles above Silver City, local worthies at the time considered themselves to be in a Provisional Territory of Arizona. This consisted of the parts of present-day New Mexico *and* Arizona south of the latitude line 33° 40', which lay several miles north of Fort Craig on the Rio Grande. Delegates to the conference that created this rump territory consisted of promoters with a varity of interests, a few army officers, merchants, a journalist or two and at least one attorney. They had met in Tucson in early April, 1860, and adopted a provisional constitution; subsequently they elected a governor and appointed other territorial officials as well.[6] People in Pino Alto were fully in agreement with these proceedings. In Washington DC, an indifferent Congress slumbered on.

The first stampede to Pino Alto was described by Hank Smith, who gave a vivid account of a shootout at George Caldwell's Fandango and Gambling House, apparently an event that never happened, however. This was not mentioned in any known contemporary source. Smith continued with a tale about another shoot-em-up, this one between Bill Dick and Will Taylor in Bill Thatcher's Fandango and Gambling Hall, a story that the best-known history of early Pino Also mentioned.[7]

This time not only did the bullets fly, but Hank Smith's recollection that "for about five minutes it seemed a perfect hell between the screams of the women and the groans of wounded and dying men" might even be an understatement. Thanks to *The Mesilla Times,* we have graphic accounts of not only the gunfight, the incarceration, and charges made against the accused murderers, but the abrupt conclusion almost two months later when the rough hand of frontier justice settled matters once and for all. Here, from four issues of the newspaper, is the entire story:

"Murder at Pino Alto"

We are this week called upon to chronicle a most sad and heart-rending event—one which has cast a general gloom over our community. On Thursday night, November 1, at a Baile given in Pino Alto, Mr. Wm. Dack (*sic*), a well-known and highly respected citizen, who has resided in our midst some time, was almost instantly killed, and three other men wounded—two probably mortally. The following particulars of the affray we have gathered from Mr. Catlett who was present at the trial:

It appears that sometime last winter Mr. Dack and Mr. Taylor had some trouble at this place, and that hard feelings have existed between them ever since. This old matter probably led to the tragic scene we are about to record. On the evening in question, Mr. Thatcher, who was in attendance at the Baile room, stepped up to the bar and called upon all present to come up and drink, remarked as he did so that he believed all present were his friends. Mr. Dack advancing towards the bar said, "Say that again, I want to hear it!" Whereupon Taylor, who was present, cried out "Let the damned scoundrel come, I will get him!" and immediately drew his pistol, leveled it at him and fired. It is supposed, however that the ball went into the air, as the pistol was thrown out of range by an individual standing near.

Wrenching himself from the grasp of those who were attempting to hold him, he fired at Dack the second time, the ball probably taking effect. Almost simultaneously with this shot, three others were fired into Dack's person. He had now evidently received his mortal wound; but, as he sunk down, he reeled to a post and grasped it with his left arm while he drew his pistol with his right hand, and fired at Taylor, the ball taking effect in his thigh. He then fell over dead, without a groan or exclamation of any kind. Two other shots were afterwards fired into his body from a Dragoon pistol in the hands of Chas. Hampton. Altogether, he received eight balls in his person—one in the arm, five in the breast, one in the thigh, and one in the abdomen—besides one wound with a knife.

Subsequently Mr. Thatcher pointed out Charles Hampton as one of the murderers, which the latter pronounced a damned lie, and fired at the former with his six shooter, but missed him and shot Mr. Wright of De Witte, Texas, through the mouth. Hampton then attempted to escape through the back door and in so doing was shot twice by parties in the room, the balls both lodging in his head.

According to the evidence presented at the trial, Taylor fired two shots, Edward Coulbert two, Colonel Sterten one, and a man with a blue shirt, not yet recognized, three shots.

Taylor and Hampton are very dangerously and, it is believed by many, mortally wounded. Wright, though suffering considerably, is not seriously injured.

We, the jury find the following verdict: When Walter Taylor and Charles Hampton have recovered sufficiently in the estimation of their Physicians to travel, they shall be banished from New Mexico and Arizona and if again caught within their limits to be hung. Colonel Sterten and Mr. Coulbert are requested to leave the country and not be caught again in either Arizona or New Mexico.

Mr. Sterten is now at Fort Webster and claims protection from the Military. Mr. Coulbert escaped from those who had him in charge, after sentence had been passed upon him. He was fired at twice and from his action it was supposed one of the balls took effect, but we have not learned of his being seen since.

Thus, we have given a brief account of the first murder that has ever occurred at the Pino Alto Mines, and we trust this is the last we shall be called upon to record. We learn great excitement was manifested by the citizens of Pino Alto on the morning subsequent to the murder, and that it was with difficulty they were restrained from hanging the prisoners forthwith. No regular business was attended to and nothing else was talked of.[8]

Charles. Hampton and Colonel Sterten, implicated in the murder of William. Dack, are now in confinement. Coulbert is supposed to have gone toward Santa Fe. The blue shirt man was seen at Apache Pass. Taylor has evaded arrest so far, but is reported secreted in the neighborhood of Pino Alto, being unable to ride, even in a buggy.[9]

An examination was held before Squire Navarrez, at Las Cruces, on the 27th inst., of Colonel Sterten, Chas. Hampton and Coulbert who were arrested for the murder of Wm. Dick at Pino Alto. Hon. P.T. Herbert appeared as counsel for the prosecution and W. Claude Jones and Colonel McWillie for the defense. The accused were committed to answer the charge of murder in the first degree at the next term of the District Court.[10]

Last Sunday night, between the hours of eight and nine the door of the building in which Mr. Coulbert, Chas. Hampton, and Colonel Sterten have been for some time confined on a charge of murder at Pino Alto, was broken open and the two latter shot dead and the former wounded in the right arm and breast. The person who was left in charge of the prisoners had chained them to a post and then gone down town for a few moments, supposing them perfectly safe. The murderers, probably believing they had killed them all, fled. Mr. Coulbert, stimulated by fear and excitement, succeeded in breaking the lock with which he was confined and, leaving the building, proceeded in the direction of Mr. Lucas' house as fast as his manacled limbs and wounds would permit and on the way met some individual to whom he gave information of the assault.

A number of men soon collected around the house where the two prisoners lay dead and still in irons, and Dr. Black was called and dressed Coulbert's wounds. From some course not clearly understood, the citizens soon dispersed, leaving two gentlemen in charge of the surviving prisoner and the bodies of his companions. In a few minutes after, both the two men on guard came across the Plaza on the run stating that the prisoner said his wounds pained him very much and earnestly requested them to make all haste and get the Doctor. On returning, Coulbert could not be found. Considerable search was made for him that night, but no clue to his whereabouts could be obtained.

The next morning, Dr. Black, who resides in a house adjoining, stated that "his lady" heard the prisoner pass down the street by their house immediately after the guard left begging, the while, that his life might be spared; and that soon after she heard several shots fired further down the street in the direction he was going. About 8 o'clock in the morning a Mexican from 'California' stated that the prisoner was on that side of the Acequia Madre, in a *jacal,* badly wounded. On repairing thence, he was found as stated, and although suffering from several severe wounds, and the cold, was able to sit up and converse.

He however appeared loath to say much regarding the unhappy affair of the previous evening, but since then he has so far recovered from his fright and the excitement as to be induced to make some further disclosures in regard to this dastardly murder and outrage upon this community. He says he left the room as soon as the two men on guard started away but had proceeded only a short distance when he was waylaid by two men who fired at him several times, two balls taking effect. He instantly fell as though mortally wounded, when one of the assassins, probably supposing him to be in the agonies of death, came up and kicked him, exclaiming, "D---n you, you are dead now," or in words to that effect, after which, having placed his hand on his temple to ascertain if he was still alive, quickly disappeared.

As soon as he considered it safe, he got up and, though suffering from his wounds, hand-cuffed and shackled, hobbled across the *acequia* and entered the *jacal* where he was found in the morning. Dr. Black was summoned, who had his manacles removed, dressed his wounds, and had him conveyed to his own house, where he still remains, though we believe it is the intention to remove him to Fort Fillmore soon, for surgical treatment and better protection.

Thus we have very briefly stated the particulars of a double murder of the most cold-blooded and dastardly character. The murder of the miners, and for which the prisoners were in confinement, was horrible, God knows, but nothing in comparison with this, that, so far as these three prisoners were concerned, was probably done under the influence of excitement and the crazing effects of liquor; this was premeditated and accomplished by heartless men, before whose base acts hell itself would pale with horror, for no others could be guilty of a crime so heinous.

Our citizens are very indignant, and take no pains to hide their feelings and opinions, though all appear cool and collected. May Wisdom guide their acts is our earnest prayer.[11]

And the man with the blue shirt was seen no more.

Southern New Mexico at this period was home to a parade of colorful characters, including James Tevis, Hank Smith, Jack Swilling, W. Claude Jones, P.T. Herbert, and M.N. MacWillie.[12] The principals in this case of multiple murders are less well known but a few details can be found in the 1860 Census schedule.

Benjamin Neal, the lawyer, at age 45 was one of the older persons in Pino Alto. He was also the attorney general in the Provisional Government of the Territory of Arizona. Judge Holt, the Justice of the Peace, apparently held his office under the same government, and references to the District Court would refer to the provisional Territory of Arizona rather than to New Mexico Territory. Whether this district court was ever constituted or convened is not known.

Colonel Sterten was A.G. Sterten, age 31, a native of Norway. The Fort Webster where he sought protection was not the post of that name from the early 1850s but an early reference to Fort McLane, established at Apache Tejo south of modern Bayard, New Mexico, in the fall of 1860.[13] Sterten was a miner, but a few years earlier he, along with James Tevis and probably others in the Pino Alto community, had joined William Walker's filibusters in Nicaragua. This was the source of their assumed military titles, although nothing indicates that any of them were officers at that time. Walker himself had been shot by a firing squad in Honduras scarcely seven weeks before the fracas in Pino Alto; newspapers at the time were full of stories about his more recent exploits and then his execution.

Charles Hampton, a 29-year-old miner from Virginia, shared a dwelling (#1171) with Neal and Sterten. The latter member of this trio had a modest personal estate, but at $15,000, Hampton's holdings made him one of the wealthiest men in Pino Alto. He of course did not live to enjoy it.

Edward Coulbert was not wounded in the original exchange of gunfire, but he narrowly escaped death twice in Mesilla. He was a New Yorker, 27 years of age, and a wheelwright by trade. Perhaps he was one of the Overland Mail Company employees who left for the mines during June, though we are told that nearly all of them recovered from gold fever and returned to duty.[14]

Walter Taylor, who started it all, collected a bullet in his thigh but otherwise came out of this affair better than anyone except for the man in the blue shirt. Taylor was another miner, from Maryland and 31 years old. He shared a house in Pino Alto with Jacob Snively, but made himself scarce after November 1st. Hank Smith said that Taylor was laid up for about six months with his leg injury; another writer said that he escaped to Old Mexico and was thought to be living near Corralitos.[15]

The newspaper didn't identify the Baile room which, according to Hank Smith, was Bill Thatcher's Fandango and Gambling Hall. At 25, **W.H. Thatcher** was the youngest of anyone in this melee. He gave his occupation as "gentleman" to the census-taker, though he was of modest means ($1,000 estate). Thatcher evidently had a knack for saying the wrong thing, but he was lucky that Charles Hampton's aim was poor and the bullet missed.

William Dack (*sic,* **Dick**) was not listed in the Pino Alto census and we know very little about him. Hank Smith said that Dick was a Superintendent of the Overland Mail Company, but this was evidently not so.[16] His name is not found in references about this cross-country stage line and he was not listed in the census returns for Overland Mail Company personnel in Arizona or Doña Ana counties. From the newspapers we know that Giles Hawley was Superintendent of the sixth division, between El Paso and Tucson. Dick was a "well-known and highly respected citizen," at least to *The Mesilla Times,* and the trouble started because of a grudge that Taylor had nursed since the previous winter over something that had happened at Mesilla. The fact that three individuals besides Taylor used Dick for target practice suggests that there was more to it than this. The jurors in Pino Alto and Judge Holt in Mesilla, who rendered the final verdict, seemed to agree with the newspaper that the whole affair "was premeditated and accomplished by heartless men."

About this time the first quartz lode (the Pacific mine) was located and individual violence faded as the miners' attention shifted from placers to more capital-intensive and less free-for-all hard rock mining. Within a year nearly all of the miners were gone, drawn away by the unfolding of the Civil War, but in time Pinos Altos would boom again.

14. Buckhorn Saloon at Pinos Altos, since 1865. Juliet White, Only in Your State.

15. Placer miner near Pinos Altos, c. 1940. Russell Lee photograph, Library of Congress.

NOTES

1. National Archives Microfilm Publications, Microcopy 653 (1967), Population Schedules of the Eighth Census of the United States, 1860, Roll 712. New Mexico, Vol. 1.

2. *Rocky Mountain News* (Denver), August 29, 1860, p. 1; *The San Francisco Herald,* September 8, 1860, p. 3.

3. *The Ranchero* (Corpus Christi, Texas), November 3, 1860, p. 2.

4. Tevis, James H. Tevis. *Arizona in the '50s.* Albuquerque: University of New Mexico Press (1954) p. 198.

5. *The Mesilla Times,* November 1, 1860, p. 2.

6. Sacks, B. *Be It Enacted: The Creation of the Territory of Arizona.* Phoenix: Arizona Historical Foundation (1964) pp. 35-42.

7. Anderson, Hattie M. editor. "Mining and Indian Fighting in Arizona and New Mexico, 1858–1861: Memoirs of Hank Smith." *Panhandle-Plains Historical Review,* Vol 1(1928), p. 92-93; R.S. Allen, "Pinos Altos, New Mexico," *New Mexico Historical Review* 23(4), October 1948, pp. 304-305.

8. *Santa-Fe Gazette,* November 24, 1860, p. 2, quoting *The Mesilla Times* of November 8, 1860.

9. *The San Francisco Herald,* November 27, 1860, p. 2, quoting *The Mesilla Times* of November 15, 1860.

10. *Daily Alta California* (San Francisco), December 14, 1860, p. 1, quoting *The Mesilla Times* of November 29, 1860.

11. *Santa Fe Gazette,* January 19, 1861, quoting *The Mesilla Times* of January 3, 1861.

12. See B. Sacks, Note 6 above, for more details.

13. Frazer, Robert W. *Forts of the West.* Norman, University of Oklahoma Press (1965), p. 100.

14. *Daily Alta California,* July 25, 1860 p. 1; *The Ranchero* (Corpus Christi,

Texas), August 4, 1860, p. 2.

15. Anderson, "Memoirs of Hank Smith," p. 93; Allen, "Pinos Altos," p. 305.

16. Anderson, "Memoirs of Hank Smith," p.93.

This chapter has been rewritten from its original appearance in *La Crónica de Nuevo México,* No. 40 (April 1995), where the title "Murder Most Foul" was used on page 1. It was later reprinted in *Sunshine and Shadows in New Mexico's Past,* Vol. II (2011). Los Ranchos: Rio Grande Books.

~ 6 ~

FROM STAGE TO PONY TO TALKING WIRE

ACROSS THE COUNTRY IN 1860

A NEW ERA IN CROSS-COUNTRY COMMUNICATIONS OPENED IN OCTOBER 1858, when the Butterfield Overland Mail linked the westernmost railroad line in Missouri with San Francisco in California. The stagecoaches and celerity wagons completed their 2,800 mile runs in as little as twenty-one days. The westbound coaches entered New Mexico twice; once at Crow Flats, west of the Pecos River, and again from El Paso, to continue through Mesilla to Cooke's Spring, Mowry City, and Soldier's Farewell to Doubtful Canyon, a few miles north of modern Interstate 10 on what would become the boundary with Arizona. From there they rolled on through Apache Pass, Dragoon Springs, Tucson, Picacho Pass, Maricopa Wells and Gila Bend to Fort Yuma and beyond. Then in early March of 1861, with the onset of the Civil War, Congress annulled Butterfield's mail subsidy and ended service on this route.

In the meantime, the famous Pony Express began service in April 1860 along what was called the central overland route, through Nebraska, Wyoming, Utah and Nevada. Their express riders rode relays between 190 or so way-stations, from St. Joseph, Missouri, to Sacramento, California. They reduced the time required by Butterfield's coaches by half, over a distance of just under 2,000 miles. Although immensely popular at the time, the privately-funded Pony Express could carry relatively few letters and at a very expensive rate. This venture went bankrupt after it ceased operation in October 1861.

The newest wonder of the age, the Pacific Telegraph Company, replaced the Pony Express. The telegraph also followed the central route as it brought the coasts of our country closer together than at any time before. The first message transmitted by wire from Sacramento reached President Abraham Lincoln in Washington DC on October 25, 1861, in an elapsed time of only fifteen hours and fifty minutes. The telegraph required relays and could transmit only one message at a time, but on the first day more than 200 messages passed over the single line. Communications that required three weeks in 1858 needed less than a day just three years later.

The Butterfield Overland Mail and the Pony Express maintained their schedules well, although both met with occasional delays due to rivers in flood and unfriendly Indians. The arrival of the talking wire brought a new problem, one we might even think of as equivalent to a computer virus. The equipment was not at fault, nor were humans responsible. Instead, nature intervened in a way that no one could have expected. The *Palmyra* (Missouri) *Spectator* gave this account of what happened.

"The buffaloes find in the telegraph poles on the overland line a new source of delight on the treeless prairie—the novelty of having something to scratch against. But, it was expensive scratching for the telegraph company, and there, indeed, was the rub, for the bison shook down miles of wire daily. A bright idea struck somebody to send to St. Louis and Chicago for all the bradawls that could be purchased, and these were driven into the poles with a view to wound the animals and check their rubbing propensity. Never was a greater mistake made. The buffaloes were delighted. For the first time they came to the scratch sure of a sensation in their thick hides that thrilled them from horn to tail. They would go fifteen miles to find a bradawl!"

Bradawls, at one time common tools in cabinetry and furniture-making, were thin rods having a chisel point at one end, normally used with a wooden handle. How the telegraph company resolved its problem, we are not told. Today, an idea equivalent to the bradawls might be someone's ticket to a CEO position. At least until the buffalos arrived.

REFERENCES

Conkling, Roscoe P. and Margaret B. *The Butterfield Overland Mail, 1857–1869*, 3 vols. Glendale, Ca.: The Arthur H. Clark Co. (1947).

Hardesty, Donald L. *The Pony Express in Central Nevada*. Bureau of Land Management, Nevada State Office, Cultural Resource Series No. 1 (1979).

The New York Times, October 26, 1861, p. 4; October 27, 1861, p. 5; October 29, 1861, p. 5.

Palmyra Spectator (Palmyra, Missouri), April 16, 1869, page 1.

Web sites for the Pony Express.

~ 7 ~

A SKETCH OF FORT MCRAE

(AND A MONTH IN RESIDENCE)

DURING HIS FOUR YEARS (1862–1866) AS COMMANDER OF THE MILITARY Department of New Mexico, Brigadier General James H. Carleton created at least six new military forts and reestablished or caused to be rebuilt several others. This amounted to more activity than at any time since troops were moved out of the towns back in 1851–1852. Among the six new posts was Fort McRae, officially established on 3 April 1863, named in honor of Captain Alexander McRae, 3rd U.S Cavalry, killed 21 February 1862 in the Battle of Valverde, New Mexico. The nominal purpose of the new garrison was to afford protection against Apache depredations at the nearby Rio Grande settlements and to aid travelers on the Jornada del Muerto to the east.

The post lay in a strategic location—near a good spring within a canyon that formed a pass between two mountain ranges. McRae Canyon linked the Rio Grande valley some two miles to the west with the major route of north-south travel in the jornada to the east. The first garrisons were volunteer troops raised for service during the Civil War, who served until regular army infantry troops took station there in 1866. The troop strength was never very large—a company or two—although a respectable physical plant grew up over the years. The site today is even more remote than it was 150 years ago, since it is accessible from the east only through White Sands Missile Range and from the west by boat across Elephant Butte Reservoir. This has helped to preserve it from the ravages of vandalism although it has been flooded by high waters on occasion. The stone walls of the hay yard still stand while other structures have been reduced to low foundations.

The fort began as a tent camp, with permanent construction deferred until 1865, followed by later additions. In a letter to his brother on October 24, 1863, the post commander Captain Albert J. Fountain described his own quarters: "We are very comfortably situated here. My quarters consist of two rooms of a circular form, each about 15 feet in diameter. These are made by setting logs in the ground to a height of 15 feet and plastered on the inside with clay; above, for a roof, is a Sibley tent held up by a tripod of poles on the outside. One of these rooms has a fire place and is used as a sitting room, office &c. The other is a bedroom. The furniture consists of chairs and tables of hewn cottonwood timber. ... Close by the door hangs my saddle, a "Californian," over it my rifle, a Sharps Breechloader, and my revolvers, Colt's Improved Dragoon size. On the other side are riding boots, spurs, wraps(?), lariats, Bowie knives, saddle bags, canteens—all arranged ready for a moment's warning."

The post-1870 work was evidently well-done and maintenance kept up; reports in 1870 and 1876 used the seldom-seen adjectives "excellent" and "good condition" with reference to the buildings. The 1870 Surgeon General's Report on Barracks and Hospitals carried a description of the post while comprehensive maps of the fort and its reservation are in the 1876 compilation. Two valuable sketches of the post may be seen in Herbert Hart's 1967 Pioneer Forts of the West; an obviously earlier one that shows jacal structures (page 7) and another (page 183) made after most of the permanent buildings had been built.

In 1885, nine years after its abandonment, Captain Thomas Branigan of the Mescalero Indian reservation police reported that the old post was badly dilapidated and also that...

The cemetery contains about thirty graves, the inmates of nearly all being killed by the Apaches. In the center of the graveyard is a neat and pretty monument, nine feet high, erected to the memory of the colored volunteers, by surviving comrades.

This monument might pertain to units of the 38th Infantry or the 125th U.S. Colored Infantry, stationed there from 1866 through 1869, or to Company B, 9th U.S. Cavalry during its ten-month tour in 1875–1876.

One of the burials in the post cemetery is that of Corporal Frank Bratling, 8th U.S. Cavalry, killed on July 8th, 1873, in a fierce fight with Apache Indians about thirty-five miles northwest of Fort McRae. This came about when Captain George Chilson led ten men in a patrol out of Fort Selden in pursuit of Apache Indians who had driven off horses from Knight's ranch. He caught up with them in a canyon, where…

They…were soon discovered…and riding up on a hill overlooking the cañon to within about 20 paces [of the Indians] I ordered the men to dismount and fight on foot. One Indian was soon dispatched and was found on examination to have 6 bullet holes in his body. At this point one of my men, Corpl. Frank Bratling "C"Troop 8th Cav., while kneeling to take more deliberate aim and in open ground within 20 paces of the Indians, was shot through the heart and instantly killed.

Three of the Indians were killed and a dozen horses recovered. Bratling's body was returned to Fort McRae and buried there on July 14th, alongside others who had died at that post. Bratling subsequently was awarded the Medal of Honor. All those in the cemetery remain there today.

Just ten years earlier, at a time when the Mescalero Apaches were supposedly being held at the Bosque Redondo reservation on the Pecos River, Captain Albert Pfeiffer and his family were attacked by fifteen or twenty Indians when he sought relief for his rheumatic pains in the warm springs eight miles from Fort McRae, at what is now Truth or Consequences, New Mexico. With him were his wife, two servant girls, and a bodyguard of six New Mexico Volunteers. Two men in the escort were killed; Pfeiffer and a civilian with them were wounded, while Mrs. Pfeiffer and one of the servant girls were carried away and then left along the trail, badly wounded. They also died. Pfeiffer, an officer in the 1st New Mexico Volunteers, thereafter became a dedicated Indian hunter.

Two years later in the fort's history, Captain William F. Ffrench and his Co D, 1st Battalion of Veteran Infantry, California, served at the post from February 1865 through July 1866. They probably erected roughly half of the buildings. Ffrench submitted the report given below a few months after their arrival, when construction was well along, floods excepted. At the same time, the captain was trying to maintain a military presence among the Apaches, sending out scouting parties and posting detachments elsewhere, which drew heavily on his resources. His success with the building program is evident from his subsequent descriptions, except that the "picket" [jacal] quartermaster and commissary storehouse apparently had a short life; the 1870 report implied that a new, adobe-built structure housed those functions.

Captain Ffrench's use of names can be made more explicit. La Cañada or Cañada was Cañada Alamosa, a new community on the stream of the same name, now known as Monticello. It replaced two earlier settlements, the first called Alamosa and the second New Alamosa or Alamocita, along the Rio Grande just below the mouth of the Cañada. The ford across the Rio Grande that he called San Diego Crossing lay about half-way between old Fort Thorn and Fort Selden, below Tonuco Montain. His Lookout Mountain is not identified. Alamosa in 1865 would have been New Alamosa, six miles from the fort and upstream on the east side of the river. By "Lieut. Slater" he meant 1st Lieutenant John Slater of his own company, like Ffrench a veteran of the 5th Infantry California Volunteers. A photocopy of Captain Ffrench's report, his "month at Fort McRae," is in the Bosque Redondo file, Schroeder Collection at the New Mexico State Records Center and Archives in Santa Fe. The cooperation of the records center is most appreciated. Ffrench's original spelling and abbreviations have been retained.

Fort McRae, N.M.

July 23d, 1865

Major,

In compliance with requirement of letter, (autograph) from the General Commanding the Department, received 18th inst., I have the honor to submit the following.

Report of operations from this Post, having for their object the capture or punishment of Indians, from June 18th to present date.

June 18th – 2 N.C. Offr's & 10 Privates sent to La Cañada N.M. to protect that settlement from future Indian depredations. Weekly report received from thence yesterday. No depradations since posting this detachment.

June 21st – Advices of the escape of some Navajoes from the Reservation received. One Lieut. One NC. Officer and Nine Privates sent as Scout, to patrol the river, south of the post to San Diego Crossing. The Picket Guard at Lookout Mountain, on the Jornada, reinforced.

June 26th – 1 Lieut. 2 N.C. Offr's & 8 Privates sent to scout down the Jornada, to Point of Rocks, thence to San Diego Crossing across and up the river back to the post.

July 3d – 1 Captain (myself) 1 N.C. Off"r & 9 Privates, sent across the river, to cooperate with Lieut. Slater's detachment sent same day, in rapid pursuit of a party of Indians reported in a Cañon, S.E. and about six miles from the post, with view to capture, or force them across the river, to be intercepted by the detachment under my command.

July 13th – 2 Lieuts. 1 N.C. Off'r & 10 Privates, sent in pursuit of Indians seen late in the evening about 5 miles below the post, after the first detachment had passed that point.

Reports of these last two details, made to Dept. Head Qrs. July 14th 1865.

I would respectfully state, that the utmost vigilance was exercised, and the best in my judgment was done to intercept and capture the runaway Indians, and I am fully convinced that our operations had the effect of checking the Indians, preventing their escape across the river in the neighborhood, causing them to return in the direction from which they came and although apparently nothing has been accomplished, it is evident that the Indians were exceedingly cautious, and very much in dread of our scouts, as I have been informed since by one José Pillon, an escaped Navajo, who was with the party last pursued, and who surrendered himself on the 17th inst. No report of these operations would have been made, if not called for, as I, as well as my command, feel very much chagrined, that our best endeavors have been apparently barren of results. The details for the scouts were made from a total of 49 enlisted men present during the past month, the duties of the post, and the improvements not being interrupted, no time being lost, nor anyone without continuous occupation or employment.

Report of the number of fighting men, and serviceable horses at Fort McRae, N.M.

Fort McRae, N.M. July 23d 1865	Captains	Lieutenants	Enlisted Men	Aggregate	Com'd Officers	Enlisted Men	Aggregate	Aggregate present & absent	Horses Serviceable	Unserviceable	Total	Rem'ks
On Det. Service	/	/	/	/	1	27	28	/	8	/	8	
Present, Sick	/	/	2	2	/	/	/	/	/	/	/	
"in confinement	/	/	1	1	/	/	/	/	/	/	/	
" for duty	1	1	46	48	/	/	/	/	22	4	26	
"casually at Post.	/	1	/	1	/	/	/	/	/	/	/	Lt. Rhodes
Total	1	2	49	52	1	27	28	80	30	4	34	

Of the 4 uns'ble horses, 2 are mares with young colts, 1 small mare, and 1 small horse in poor condition not suitable for service when in good condition, the serviceable horses are very thin, and 3 of them, as I am informed, have had sore backs, ever since they came to the post. The horses are Kept on pasture daily, from 6:30 A.M. to 7 P.M., they are well groomed, and are fed grama hay at night, but miss the grain forage so much that from very fine, they have fallen into poor condition.

Report of the prospects of the harvest in the neighborhood of Fort McRae.

The Wheat, now being cut, is not as good as expected, not much over a half crop will be harvested, and very little to be purchased.

The Corn. Is very fine, so far without damage, and to the extent of the planting, promises a good yield.

In regard to the progress in building, I would respectfully state, that the Quartermaster and Commissary Storehouse, picket building [i.e., *jacal*] 24 x 50 feet, 10 feet height in the clear, is complete, and contains the property of those departments. The Stable for 40 horses lacks the roof over the stalls.

The Company quarters, 2 squad rooms each 24 x 50 ft. mess room 22 x 50 ft. Orderly Serg^{ts} and Company storeroom of adobe, is ready for the vegas [*vigas*], the doors and window sashes made at the post are nearly all finished, this quarters will be ready for occupancy early next month. Tomorrow morning the Hospital, of adobe, will be commenced, all these improvements will be urged to completion as rapidly as the means allowed will permit. This work was commenced on the 9th May last, 2 Carpenters, 4 Masons and 10 Laborers /duly authorized/ being employed. It was directed to build picket quarters, hospital storerooms &c, accordingly the major portion of the timbers were fallen, but the river overflowing suddenly, they were buried up, and floated off, before they could be hauled out, thus embarrassing the projected improvements.

It was ascertained when building the picket store house, that an adobe building could be constructed quicker and cheaper, than cutting, hauling and setting up pickets, daubing them inside and out with mud, and competing a building of that character, which is neither as sightly, secure, comfortable, or durable, as an adobe one. Accordingly, it was decided to build of adobe, and I am sure the General would be pleased with the contrast which even now exists between the former and present appearances of the post. The timbers, very fine ones, are gotten out by men of my company and details from it are made daily to assist in the improvements. The cost of labor /the greatest expense, since the materials are procured by the hired labor/ is $640 per month, and I respectfully venture to say, that no buildings or improvements equally good are being or can be made as economically at any post in the territory.

I am very respectfully

Your obed^t servant,

Major B.C. Cutler Wm. F. Ffrench,
Asst. Adjt. Gen'l   Capt. 1st Vet. Inf. C.V.
Dept. New Mexico,   Com'g Post.

Santa Fe, N.M.

16. Fort McRae, View from the Guardhouse; soldier's sketch c. 1871. U.S. National Archives and Records Service.

FRANK FRENGER,
SUTLER AT
FORT M^cRAE, N.M.,
Keeps constantly on hand all articles useful to PROSPECTORS, MINERS, and TRA-VELERS; which he will sell cheap. Give him a call.   193y

17. Sutler's advertisement, Fort McRae. *The Albuquerque Press,* February 9, 1867.

REFERENCES

Agnew, S.C. 1971 *Garrisons of the Regular U.S. Army, New Mexico, 1846–1899*. Santa Fe: The Press of the Territorian.

Hart, Herbert M. 1967 *Pioneer Forts of the West*. Seattle: Superior Publishing Company.

Keleher, William A. *The Fabulous Frontier, 1846–1912*, 1962. Albuquerque: University of New Mexico Press. New Edition, Santa Fe: Sunstone Press, 2008.

Albert J. Fountain, letter of October 24, 1863. to Dear Brother. Photostat copy in University of Arizona Special Collections Library, Maurice Fulton Papers, Box 11 Folder 7.

New Mexico State Records Center and Archives. Mescalero Apache File (1859–1875), Schroeder Collection (photocopies of documents from the National Archives, Record Group 98)

Orton, Richard H. (compiler) 1890 *Records of California Men in the War of the Rebellion, 1861 to 1867*. Sacramento.

U.S. National Archives. Microcopy M1088 – Letters Received by Headquarters District of New Mexico, September 1865–August 1890, Roll 20, File No. S-55.

U.S. War Department, Military Division of the Missouri 1876 *Outline Descriptions of the Posts in the Military Division of the Missouri,* et. al. (reprinted 1969). Washington, DC.

U.S. War Department, Surgeon-General's Office 1870 *A Report on Barracks and Hospitals with Descriptions of Military Posts*. Washington, DC.

~ 8 ~

A TRIP TO THE SILVER MINES

"All seated?""Yes, all right, go ahead!"The gray leaders plunge."Kentuck," the
messenger, toots a toot of "Up in a balloon, boys," upon his battered brass horn,
and away we are. Going "out-west" to see our neighbors![1]

ON THIS EXUBERANT NOTE THE SOON-TO-BE EDITOR OF THE LAS CRUCES, NEW
Mexico newspaper *The Borderer* whirled off on his brother's Southern Overland
Mail and Express Line "on a sociable trip" to visit the neighbors in Silver
City some 140 miles distant. It was mid-winter of 1871 and the passenger,
Nehemiah V. Bennett, had been a resident of the Mesilla Valley since 1868.
His brother, Joseph F. Bennett, a partner in the stage line, had arrived earlier
with the California Column during the Civil War. Joseph's encouragement
prompted Nehemiah to come west for his health. The brother proved to be
a talented newsman, and for four and a half years his paper fulfilled its early
promise of becoming one of southern New Mexico's most vigorous weeklies.[2]

The trip to Silver City amounted to a subscription-raising jaunt with
Nehemiah keeping up a lively travelogue along the way, commenting on
whatever caught his eye. Once underway, the coach…

…rushed by the beautiful and level fields on either side of the road
where the rancheros are busily engaged in sowing crops, and we
are upon the river's [Rio Grande] banks, waiting for the horseman
who has accompanied us to cross and see if the ford is the same [as]
yesterday. Were it not for this precaution our leaders might plunge
out of sight in some deep hole, and go under—giving us (the only
passenger) a right smart chance of ducking in the bargain.

Safely across the river, they were off again…

…up a long sandy hill for full three miles, and then over a level plain and road, as hard and smooth as plank. Mid-winter—yet the grass stands knee-high all over the plain, partially cured by nature. Examine it, and almost every stalk is alive, and with [the] returning rainy season will be as green as ever.

Bennett glimpsed the country as it appeared before herds of cattle ranged over the desert grasslands, when the only livestock were animals being driven west to California. He saw the landscape as a series of discoveries:

An immense plain, so completely diversified with immense mountains, that we almost consider ourselves hemmed in on every side; but examine them closely, and we can discover from the base— far up the side of some of them—the outline of huge cañons; can even see the trees that, in many instances, mark the line of springs or the course of rushing water during the rainy season while the others and more distant ones present to us the beautiful tints of purple and azure that so delight us in pictures. We may ride all day with the road making a straight line for some high mountain that throws its ragged peaks above the clouds, wondering what we shall do when we reach its base; but, distance decreases and we get near enough to distinguish its openings, a slight deviation to the right or left shows us a wide valley through what we have been all day considering an impassible barrier to further progress.

All of this may sound very foreign to a modern traveler on Interstate 10, but even today a back country journey via the ranch roads allows one to recapture part of the sense of what it was like 150 years ago. Bennett's coach followed the old Overland Mail route, which lies north of the modern Interstate, to their first stop about twenty-five miles west of Las Cruces.

A steady trot…has brought us to Slocum's Ranch. Who doesn't know

Slocum? If you do not, dear reader, the first time you trip it to the mines, you will be sure to stop and make his acquaintance, for it is the only watering place for many a long mile. Slocum (an old California volunteer) believed that by digging immense tanks at this place, enough water could be secured for travelers all the year round, and he has succeeded, and also built up a good house, and large and excellent stables and corrals.

John D. Slocum, who had reenlisted in the 1st Veteran Infantry, California Volunteers, mustered out in 1866. By 1869 he had built Slocum's Ranch, the only watering place between the Rio Grande and Fort Cummings, a day's journey west of the Mesilla Valley on the road to Silver City. Emigrants could refresh themselves and also water their stock at ten cents per head. In 1875 Slocum rented his property to Richard S. Mason, who continued to operate it as a ranch and stage station into the 1880s.[3]

Stop here [Slocum's] for a meal, and you feel good-natured when you get up from the table, and the team comes from the stable very well cleaned, and looking as if they had fared as well as yourself. Another five miles brings us to the mouth of Magdalena Cañon, a quarter of a mile carries us through, yet in that short distance many a poor fellow has met his fate. A rude cross, but more frequently a pile of stones, tells us where one beloved of those whom he has left behind, was ruthlessly murdered, scalped, and perhaps tortured, while in the last agonies of death.

Bennett did not exaggerate; during the 1860s and again in 1879–1880 the southern overland route was a bloody highway. The first half of the 1870s remained comparatively peaceful, but by 1876 intermittent Indian raids had resumed. Apaches even struck at Slocum's Ranch and October 13, 1879, saw the massacre of eleven civilians at Magdalena Gap, just to the west of the ranch. The remnants of this debacle still lay scattered in the road six months later.[4] Bennett continued:

We cannot stop here to moralize. The stage whirls us over another plain around the points of other mountains, and we make Fort Cummings at midnight. A good, hot supper with Sammy Lyons, the sutler, a short chat around the stove, and that tooting horn of Kentuck's starts us out at three o'clock in the morning, to pass through the dreaded Cook's Cañon.

Fort Cummings, situated near Cooke's Spring at the eastern entrance to Cooke's Canyon. had an Army garrison from 1863 to 1873 and again from July of 1880 until October 1886.[5] Samuel J. Lyons held the post tradership beginning in 1870, apparently running a hotel and stage station as well. He continued there after the military abandoned Fort Cummings temporarily in 1873 but died along with four others about the end of May, 1880, at the hands of the Apache chief Victorio's warriors.[6]

Bennett's stage negotiated Cooke's Canyon safely and emerged into country much like what they had seen before. They rolled along to their next halt, at...

...the flourishing little town of Rio Mimbres upon the river of the same name, where once was situated (upon paper) the far-famed "Mowry City," with its magnificent steamers loading with cotton at its wharf. Since that time the volume of water has so much diminished that a common Indian canoe cannot be found upon its bosom. In fact, the "oldest inhabitant" hath no tradition that the Lo's of this section ever needed such an institution, as they could easily jump from one bank to the other, at almost any time of the year. Here we find Messrs. Newsham, St. John, and others, keeping well selected stocks of merchandise; Mr. Voorhees, a good hotel, and Messrs. Kimberlin & Co., with a fine new flouring mill. These gentlemen will, in few days, represent their town in *The Borderer* by their advertisements, when our readers will see that they are all live men.

Bennett was optimistic; the only Rio Mimbres merchant to advertise in *The Borderer* was Marshal St. John, a California Column veteran whose ad began with the June 15, 1871 issue. By 1876, St. John had moved to Doña Ana County.[7] Robert V. Newsham, another California veteran, had been the post trader at Fort Cummings in the late 1860s and later became a successful stockman, mine owner and Grant County political figure.[8] A. Voorhees is remembered as the owner of a ten or twelve-room hotel with stone walls two feet thick. Many years later the owners of the Bell Ranch remodeled this building as their headquarters.[9] Hamilton Kimberlin did place a notice in *The Borderer* as the senior partner in Kimberin and Brockman, proprietors of the water power flouring mill at Rio Mimbres.[10]

L. Boyd Finch told the story of Mowry City, the 1859–1861 predecessor of Rio Mimbres.[11] This involved a legendary print showing steamboats on the Mimbres River. No actual copy of this print has ever been seen. Mowry City came to an end in the early summer of 1861 when Indian depredations drove the settlers out of the Mimbres Valley. In 1865 or early 1866 a new settlement took root and the 1870 census reported 184 persons with 62 dwellings. Six years later, Rio Mimbres stood deserted, reportedly because farmers upstream had diverted the waters of the river.[12]

At this point [Rio Mimbres] we branch off from J. F. Bennett & Co's S.O.M. and Ex. Line, and take passage with W. H. Wiley & Co., who run a first-class branch line to Fort Bayard, Silver City and Pinos Altos. An easy-riding, open, spring wagon, giving one an opportunity to look about him in every direction; a good span of California horses; Wiley and Smith for companions, make the traveler, we can assure him, a very peasant trip over this, the most beautiful part of the country.

Five miles out we pass the celebrated Hot Spring, worthy itself of an entire article, so we give it the go-by with this brief mention, reserving it for another column. Half-way between this and Fort Bayard, we come to the site of old Fort McLean [*sic,* Fort McLane], now occupied by Mr. Bisby as a station to meet the necessities of travelers. Here is another warm spring called, we believe by the Indians, Apache Tahoo [*sic,* Apache Tejo]. With the stream flowing from this, the station is supplied, and also the garden and ranch irrigated.

A year later, Bennett did describe what he called the "Hot Springs of the Rio Mimbres."[13] The waters here, later known as Hudson Hot Springs and currently as Faywood Hot Springs, had a "house of accommodations" and bath houses as early as 1860. The customers at this early date likely would have been miners on their way to or from the new gold discoveries at Pinos Altos—or perhaps Apache warriors returning from raids into Mexico! For more than one hundred years this spring has continued to be a spa or health resort under a succession of owners.[14] The warm spring, Apache Tejo, lies just east of highway US 180 a few miles south of Hurley, New Mexico, and still bears the name (Pachiteju) of a Gila Apache chief from the 1770s.[15]

Wiley & Co.'s spring wagon hastened on to Fort Bayard, to find the officers waiting for the mail and expecting to be ordered elsewhere. Fort Bayard was less than five years old and amounted to little more than a collection of huts, built of logs and round stones.[16] Bennett mentioned the "threatened evacuation" of the post, perhaps referring to the reduction in Army strength ordered in 1870. Then another twelve miles over rolling hills brought the editor to the valley called the Cienega de San Vicente, known since 1870 as Silver City. Here, only a few months after the original silver strike, our commentator told how this was made:

For several years the valley has been the home of the Bullard brothers. Immediately back of their house stands the hill in which is located the "Legal Tender," and a great number of other mines. Over this hill they had hunted many a time without dreaming of its wealth.

Upon the receipt of news of the rich discoveries at Ralston (i.e., Shakespeare), a rush took place at once all over the country. Among the rest [were] the Bullard boys, who took a good sharp look at Ralston croppings and immediately turned for home, remarking: "If that's silver ore, we know where there's plenty of it."

The stampede to Ralston, sixty miles to the south by stage road, dates from February or March of 1870. Back in the San Vicente Valley by late May, John Bullard and seven partners located the first three claims in the Silver Flat District. Within a few months the Silver Flat and neighboring Chloride

Flat districts had merged, while six miles to the southeast of Silver City more miners staked out claims in the Lone Mountain District.

The Silver City boom was still in its early days when Bennett penned his enthusiastic description of this newest bonanza:

It is almost impossible for one to give a truthful account of the surpassing richness of these mines without laying himself open to the charge of exaggeration.

Nevertheless, he sought to do so. Hosting him at Silver City was John R. "Adobe" Johnson, active in mining and characterized as "thorough-going, industrious and energetic."[17] Two of Johnson's employees offered to subscribe to the newspaper if its proprietor would accept payment in silver.

That was good enough for us, and we ate our dinner with a relish made keen by the bright idea of getting subscriptions in the shape of silver bricks. The meal over, the boys pounded up some rock, enough we should judge, after being pounded, to make three double handfuls—kindled a fire with cedar wood, using a small Chinese bellows for blast, and in less than an hour had taken out and paid us between seven and eight dollars in pure silver We stood by and saw the whole operation, rude as it was, and wondered of the wealth that lay in that hill....

The budding editor had a good bargain, as an annual subscription to *The Borderer* amounted to $6.00. This little demonstration also pointed up the primitive conditions under which early development labored. Some of the prospect shafts had penetrated twenty to thirty feet, with one tunnel more than 100 feet in length, but as yet the miners possessed no equipment for milling their ore. Bennett continued his account of the camp:

...All are now anxiously awaiting the opening of spring, and the arrival of Mr. Carson's mill, now at Kit Carson [Colorado], or in transit from that point to its destination… Without money and almost without tools, an immense amount of work has been done. We were informed that during the fall and early winter months only three sets of miners' tools were had in the camp. Steel for drills, gads and hammers, was not to be had for any price.

For the moment, development of the town outstripped work at the prospects.

…one of the best evidences of the energy and enterprise of these men is found in the fact that Silver City, since the first day of September last, has grown from a camp of three houses to a town of over eighty nice, shingle-roofed, eastern looking buildings. The saw mill of Mr. Bremen, five miles distant, which now runs eighteen hands, keeps the supply of lumber full, and a large stock on hand (seasoning) for the summer demand.

Silver City is essentially an eastern town full of live, energetic and intelligent men who have come there to stay. There is no jumping of claims, no quarreling. The town already contains three stores, one saloon, a boarding house, livery stable, two blacksmith shops, one shoe shop, and a paint shop; and situated as it is, in the beautiful Cienega, surrounded by rolling and picturesque hills, covered with pine, cedar and oak, must in time become the most beautiful town in southern New Mexico.

With these words and a few comments about the availability of water, our editor concluded his essay on a trip to the silver mines. In later issues *The Borderer* carried many letters on the progress of mining at Ralston (renamed Shakespeare in 1879). Issues of the paper from 1871–1872 are available on microfilm, while the Special Collections at New Mexico State University had a unique opportunity to purchase fifty-some original issues of *The Borderer* dating from 1873–1874 from a bookseller and was able to do so. These have not been microfilmed. Publication of this feisty window into southern New Mexico's past suspended in September 1875.

18. Silver City in 1872. Photograph courtesy of the Silver City Museum.

J. F. BENNETT & CO'S

SOUTHERN OVERLAND
MAIL & EXPRESS LINE.

FIRST-CLASS CONCORD COACHES.

FROM SANTA FE, N. M., TO EL PASO, TEXAS, LA MESILLA, N. M., AND TUCSON, ARIZONA.

Running directly through the great Mining Districts of

RALSTON AND SILVER CITY.

Close Connections are made

AT SANTA FE, **S.** NEW MEXICO,

With Coaches for

DENVER and **O.** KIT CARSON,

On the Kansas Pacific Railroad.

AT EL PASO, **M** TEXAS,

With San Antonio and Chihuahua Coaches.

And at LA **&** MESILLA,

With Coaches for

RALSTON, TUCSON, **E.** SILVER CITY,

And all Points in

ARIZONA, SONORA, CALIFORNIA, and the PACIFIC COAST.

The Only Stage Line running south from Santa Fe through New Mexico, into Texas and Arizona.

THE BORDERER, February 7, 1872

19. Advertisement for Bennett & Co's Mail and Express Line, 1872. *The Borderer,* February 7, 1872.

SLOCUM'S RANCHE

◇——◇

The only watering between the Rio Grande and Fort Cummings.

‡——‡

I now have my large tank, 120 feet long, 20 feet wide, and 10 feet deep completed, and am prepared to water stock at reasonable rates.

My Table is supplied as well as can be in this country, and travelers will find good, clean beds:

GOOD STABLING,
HAY and GRAIN.
JOHN D. SLOCUM
22-tf.

THE HERALD, December 19, 1875

SAMUEL J. LYONS & CO.,
POST TRADERS AND
DEALERS IN MERCHANDISE,
Fort Cummings, N. M.
We have accommodation for the traveling public, and keep constantly on hand forage and wood. tf

THE BORDERER, June 15, 1871

MAIL, PASSENGER AND EXPRESS

—ROUTE FROM—

Rio Mimbres to Fort Bayard,

Pinos Altos and Silver City,

W. H. WILEY & CO.

SILVER CITY, ... NEW MEXICO.

Running in connection with J. F. Bennett & Co's P. O. Mail and Express line to Santa Fe, El Paso and Tucson.

We are prepared with First Class Outfits for carrying Passengers and Express matter between Rio Mimbres Fort Bayard, Pinos Altos and the Silver Mines. Connecting as above and making Tri-Weekly trips each way. Persons wishing to visit the richest Silver District yet discovered in the United States will find us prepared to carry them through on our line without delay.

We have also a good Livery Stable at Silver City where visitors will find everything wanted in that line. tf.

THE BORDERER, May 4, 1871

MARSHAL ST. JOHN,
—DEALER IN—
GENERAL MERCHANDISE,
GROCERIES AND PROVISIONS.
MAIN STREET, RIO MIMBRES, N. M.

THE BORDERER, June 15, 1871

A CARD.

Rio Mimbres. N. M. May 6, '71.

Mr. N. V. Bennett:

Las Cruces, N. M.

Dear Sir:—I see a notice in your paper, the Borderer, subscribed by Hugh L. Hinds, stating that he is the legal owner of a water power Flouring Mill, situated in this place; in reply to which notice you will please say in your next issue, that Hugh L. Hinds has neither title, lean or claim, whatsoever, upon any part of our Flouring Mill, and when he published above notice, H. L. Hinds knew that it was a base falsehood, and I Hamilton Kimberlin, denounce him as a liar and a swindler.

KIMBERLIN & BROCKMAN.

THE BORDERER, May 18, 1871

NOTICE

IS HEREBY GIVEN TO THE Traveling Public that I have leased the premises known as **APACHE-TU-WHOO,** formerly occupied by Mr. Tom. Feilding, and am prepared to entertain guests with the best the country affords.

DAVID SPERRY.

MINING LIFE, October 11, 1871

20. Advertisements for Southern New Mexico Businesses, 1871–1875. Local newspapers, as cited.

NOTES

1. *The Borderer* (Las Cruces, New Mexico), March 16, 1871, p. 1.

2. Miller, Darlis A. *The California Column in New Mexico.* Albuquerque: University of New Mexico Press and Historical Society of New Mexico (1982) pp. 52, 56, 130-132.

3. Miller 1982, pp. 65-66. Keith Humphries, "Trail of the Pioneers," *New Mexico Magazine,* April 1939, p. 33. Sandra L. Myers, editor, *Ho for California!* San Marino, California: Huntington Library (1980), pp. 229, 281.

4. Humphries 1939, p. 34. Miller 1982, pp. 66, 156-57. O. W. Williams, *In Old New Mexico 1879–1880*, Fort Stockton, Texas (1928), p. 12. Joseph P. Peters, *Indian Battles and Skirmishes on the American Frontier 1790–1898.* New York: Argonaut Press Ltd. (1966) p. 48. Donald Howard Couchman, *Cooke' Peak – Pasaron Por Aqui.* Las Cruces: Bureau of Land Management, Las Cruces District (1990), pp. 180, 198.

5. Couchman 1990. Lee Myers "Military Establishments in Southwestern New Mexico: Stepping Stones to Settlement," *New Mexico Historical Review* 34(1) (January 1968) pp. 29-35.

6. Peters 1966 p. 50. Couchman 1990, pp. 185-86 199, 201. Dan L. Thrapp, *Victorio and the Mimbres Apaches.* Norman: University of Oklahoma Press (1974), p. 282.

7. Miller 1982, pp. 103, 210.

8. Miller 1982, pp. 50, 59, 65, 70, 78, 103, 144, 181.

9. Bell, Olive W. "The Fabulous Frontier," *New Mexico Magazine,* June 1938, p. 42.

10. *The Borderer,* May 18, 1871, p. 2.

11. Finch, L. Boyd. *A Southwestern Land Scam: The 1859 Report of the Mowry City Association.* Tucson: Friends of the Library, University of Arizona (1990).

12. Miller 1982, pp. 102-103. Finch 1990. Isaac C. Stuck "Field Notes of the subdivision lines of Township T20S, R10W, of the principal Meridian in

the Territory of New Mexico, surveyed by Isaac C. Stuck, Dep. Sur., under contract No 31, dated June 11, 1867." New Mexico State Office, Bureau of Land Management, pp. 65-67. William A. Bell, *New Tracks in North America* (reprint of 1870 edition). Albuquerque: Horn and Wallace, Publishers (1965), pp, 261-262.

13. *The Borderer,* May 8, 1872, p. 1.

14. Bell 1965, pp. 262-264. Pat Beckett, "Casa Consuelo, New Mexico's Fountain of Age," *Rio Grande History,* No 14 (1983) pp. 2-5.

15. Wilson, John P. "The Southern Apaches as Farmers, 1630–1870," in *Reflections: Papers on Southwestern Culture History in Honor of Charles H Lange.* Papers of the Archaeological Society of New Mexico, No. 14 (1988), p. 81.

16. Reeve, Frank D., editor, "Frederick E. Phelps: A Soldier's Memoirs," *New Mexico Historical Review* 25:1 (January 1950), pp. 50-51.

17. *The Borderer,* May 18, 1871, p. 2. Helen J. Lundwall, editor, *Pioneering in Territorial Silver City.* Albuquerque: University of New Mexico Press and Historical Society of New Mexico (1983), pp. 36, 148.

This chapter has been rewritten from its original appearance in *La Crónica de Nuevo Mexico,* No. 33 (April 1992).

~ 9 ~

PILLAGING THE SILVER CITY STAGE

Robbing a stagecoach in the Old West didn't always end with the driver throwing down the express box, or a chest with the payroll or gold bars, followed by the bandits riding off and allowing everybody to go their own way. Sometimes the highwaymen sought to unburden the passengers of their money and valuables, with a little .44 caliber persuasion. This could be hazardous for the holdup men, as when a passenger on the stage westbound from Fort Yuma gave one of the outlaws who stopped it a shotgun load of buckshot in the belly. The passengers soon drove the luckless robbers away in a blazing gun battle.[1] But holdups could also end with no one being hurt, apart from monetary damages.

John Chisum was one of the most storied cattlemen of the American Southwest during the 1870s. His immense operations stretched for more than one hundred miles along the Pecos River in southeastern New Mexico, and by 1876 included his Eureka Springs Stock Ranch, a block of unoccupied federal domain in the Aravaipa Valley of southern Arizona.[2]

By this time John Chisum had become prosperous as well as prominent, and he no longer rode the range or helped trail the herds himself. In the summer of 1875 Chisum's cowboys drove 11,000 head of cattle west across the Rio Grande and through Cooke's Canyon in southern New Mexico to supply a beef contractor in Arizona. A newfound peace with the Apache Indians, following the recent closure of Fort Cummings at the eastern end of the canyon, didn't mean that travelers in that part of the Southwest went entirely unmolested.[3]

Perhaps Chisum was headed home from his Arizona holdings when three knights of the road, as the newspapers termed them, stopped the diligence [stagecoach] bearing the rancher in Cooke's Canyon, east of Silver City, New Mexico. The date was January 19, 1876. Minus some of the literary excesses favored by newspaper editors, one Las Cruces paper gave this account of what happened next.

"About 3 o'clock on Wednesday morning last, just after the diligence had ascended the steep and rugged hill at the 'Divide' in the Cañon celebrated for its many Indian fights and massacres in days of yore, the conductor fast asleep in the 'Front Boot,' the passengers, John S. Chisum of cattle notoriety and Hon. T. Conway of Santa Fe, snugly ensconced under their blankets and buffalo robes dreaming the happy hours away, three gallant Knights of the Road made their debut upon the stage and demanded an interview.

The driver obeyed the summons and informed the sleeping passengers of the somewhat unexpected nocturnal visit of the Free Lances and their polite request 'To turn the passengers out at once,' whereupon Messrs. Chisum and Conway made their appearance from under the blankets. The first objects that met their astonished gaze were the muzzles of a shotgun, Henry rifle, and a Colts revolver.

Active operations began at once; one of the robbers mounted the front boot and quickly emptied its contents on the ground, then taking a hatchet he commenced business on the express box. After the first blow on the lock the conductor surrendered the key and in a few moments some $1000 in bullion and $150 in gold coin easily and quickly changed hands; an $80 package of greenbacks fortunately escaped notice and was saved.

In the meantime, the passengers were not idle. Chisum had a sudden call to the rear of the stage and the work on transferring greenbacks from his pocketbook to the inside of his unmentionables went briskly and rapidly on until he was politely requested to return and be searched. On his return, the robbers found but $150 out of $1000 that a few moments before had been in his pocketbook, and Chisum was mean enough to beg two dollars of that for incidental expenses on the road.

Chisum's watch escaped the rapacious claws of the first Interviewer, but unfortunately another and more expert hand took the business in charge and quick as thought, Chisum's $300 watch deserted its owner.

Conway also managed to cheat the boys out of the greater part of the cash he had about his person while he fondly fancied that his watch was out of danger. The nimble searcher then began on Conway and rifled all his pockets but found no watch. Mr. Conway says he is certain the villain knew he had one; for not content with going through his pockets, the fellow began pressing out the creases and folds of his pants with his hand and he presently exclaimed 'oh,' and another $300 watch and chain had to *vamos* from its hiding place.

But the meanest and saddest part of the business is yet to be related. Last Wednesday morning was very cold up in the mountains; an indispensable article under such circumstances is a bottle of good whiskey. Well, there was just one bottle of the 'crature' in that stage. As soon as it was discovered by the robbers, Chisum, fearing the worst, proposed a drink all around. His request was at once complied with; all took a drink.

When the stage people were told to replace their baggage on the stage, C. asked for his bottle and was politely informed that he could not have it. This was too much; the unfeeling wretches would not heed his appeal, and as a last resort, he proposed a drink all around before they parted, which was acceded to. He parted with his bottle a sadder if not a wiser man. The robbers then ordered the coach to return to [Faywood] Hot Springs"—*Rio Grande Eco.*[4]

The newspaper *Eco del Rio Grande,* published in Las Cruces, New Mexico, survives as a half-dozen complete issues and scattered reprint articles, like this one, from a three-and-a-half year run (1874–1878) of what must have been an intriguing weekly. In 1878 its talented editor, Lawrence Lapoint, abandoned journalism to run a saloon, where supposedly Billy the Kid dealt *monte* for a while. Whatever else is lost, this tidbit survives to add one more window into a time when southern New Mexico was still part of the frontier.

21. John Chisum's South Spring Ranch headquarters, 1880s. University of Arizona Special Collections Library, Maurice Fulton collection.

REFERENCES

1. *The San Diego Union*, November 11 and November 18, 1869, both page 2.

2. Harwood P. Hinton, Jr., "John Simpson Chisum, 1877–1884," *New Mexico Historical Review* 31 (1956), pp. 177-205. John P. Wilson, *Islands in the Desert;* Albuquerque, University of New Mexico Press (1995), page 188.

3. Donald Howard Couchman, *Cooke's Peak – Pasaron Por Aqui*; New Mexico Bureau of Land Management, Cultural Resources Series No. 7 (1990), page 195.

4. *The Republican Review*; Albuquerque, New Mexico, January 26, 1876, page 2, reprinting from *Eco del Rio Grande*; Las Cruces, New Mexico, probably the January 22, 1876 issue.

An earlier version of this chapter appeared in *Sunshine and Shadows in New Mexico's Past,* Vol. II (2011). Los Ranchos: Rio Grande Books.

~ 10 ~

A PRIMER ON THE LINCOLN COUNTY WAR

FOR ONE YEAR, FROM FEBRUARY 18, 1878 THROUGH FEBRUARY 18, 1879, THE community of Lincoln, New Mexico witnessed one of the worst eruptions of violence in the history of the American West—the Lincoln County War. In this remote corner of southeastern New Mexico two groups fought for money and power with every means at their command, settling their differences with gunfire, until most of the leaders on one side were dead and those on the other were discredited or powerless. There were no victories or heroes and almost no one went to jail. Finally the problems just dissipated.

Lincoln began as a settlement of Hispanic farmers in the narrow valley of the Rio Bonito about the time (1855) the army established Fort Stanton some eight miles distant. Streamside plots produced surprising amounts of corn, which could be sold or traded at the army post. Then in 1871 the Mescalero Apaches made a peace agreement, settled around the fort and began to receive rations. The ration program led to a big new market for local crops.

In 1867 two Union Army veterans, Lawrence G. Murphy and Emil Fritz, formed a partnership headquartered initially at Fort Stanton. As L.G. Murphy & Co. they sought a monopoly on the sale of corn and other supplies to both the military and the Mescalero Indian agency. Many of these supplies came from local farmers, who were allowed credit at the Murphy store and in turn employed their produce to make payments. As government buyers, the fort and the Indian agency were virtually the only sources of money in this cash-poor part of the territory; wage work opportunities were scarce. The local economy depended on an elaborate series of credit arrangements, duly recorded in the ledgers of the 'House of Murphy', as the partnership was known.

For a while, Murphy and Fritz manipulated this system to their advantage, but competitive bidding for Indian supplies led them into financial difficulties. They tried to maintain a prosperous appearance even when the army kicked them out of Fort Stanton in 1873. The two partners relocated to nearby Lincoln and built the two-story Murphy-Dolan store, known later as the Lincoln County Courthouse. James Dolan replaced Emil Fritz in the partnership after Fritz' death in 1874.

Lincoln County had a tradition of violence, although the military sometimes helped to quiet matters. Then in 1875 a lawyer, Alexander McSween, and his wife Susan arrived in Lincoln and he set up a practice. His clients included pioneer cattleman John S. Chisum along the Pecos River and L.G. Murphy & Co. of Lincoln.

The following year a twenty-three-year-old Englishman, John H. Tunstall, had a casual meeting with McSween in Santa Fe. Tunstall was in search of land and business investments, and at the lawyer's invitation he came to Lincoln, arriving early in November 1876. McSween showed him how the local economy might be manipulated and within a year Tunstall had built and stocked a store, started a ranch, and even opened a bank in Lincoln. J.J. Dolan & Co., Murphy's successor, grew concerned even as that firm sank deeper into debt, while struggling to maintain appearances. Murphy and Dolan perceived Tunstall to be a real threat, especially when he began dealing with the local farmers as a prelude to bidding on government contracts.

Two factions started to form, one around Tunstall and his close associate McSween, the other around James Dolan and his new partner, John H. Riley. Murphy grew sick as time went on, but he remained a key figure in the background. Many in the community tried to remain neutral while others, including some of the leading men, farmers, ranchers, and outlaws, lined up with either party and sought to use the legal system to gain supremacy— pitting the sheriff and district court against the magistrate and his constables. This contest involved none of the traditional celluloid confrontations of a range war between big and little cattlemen, farmers vs. ranchers, or law and order against outlaws. Lincoln became a bloody battleground because of an unusual mix of personalities, the extremely limited economic opportunities, personal greed, and a refusal by all sides to back down or compromise, which led eventually to a collapse of law and order.

In February 1878 the Lincoln County Sheriff, William Brady, attached

Alexander McSween's property as part of a civil lawsuit. The sheriff included Tunstall's store and livestock as well, since he and McSween were thought to be partners. A posse that Sheriff Brady sent to Tunstall's ranch followed the young Englishman as he led a small troop of horses back towards Lincoln, catching up with him and his five ranch hands in a canyon south of the Rio Ruidoso. On February 18, 1878 three of the possemen shot him down on the spot, making Tunstall the first casualty in the Lincoln County War. Two of the accused killers were soon dead themselves while the third one, Jessie Evans, never talked. Tunstall's companions had scattered and didn't witness what actually happened.

Riding with the young rancher that day was a youth named William Bonney, who made his first recorded appearance in Lincoln one week earlier at Tunstall's store. Bonney had arrived in Lincoln County sometime in October 1877 and evidently found employment with Tunstall. Although usually at the scene of any action, it was another year before "the Kid" gained any special notice. In 1879 some called him "Billy Kid" and by the end of 1880, newspapers had given him the name we know him by today—Billy the Kid.

No one was charged in Tunstall's death. Leadership fell to McSween, but the lawyer feared for his own life and soon left Lincoln for the nearby mountains, later for John Chisum's ranch on the Pecos. Lincoln County at the time was the largest county in New Mexico and encompassed the entire southeastern part of the territory. Bands of armed men began to ride, those on McSween's side styling themselves the "Regulators." They viewed Sheriff Brady as the creature of Murphy and Dolan, and it was men in the sheriff's posse that had murdered Tunstall. The first two leaders of the Regulators, Dick Brewer and Frank McNab, also had legal status as deputy constables. In their own views, each faction represented the law.

Dolan and Riley had been forced into bankruptcy even before Tunstall's death, but they schemed to regain power with the aid of Jessie Evans and some hard-core outlaws called "the Boys," who found a place in Brady's posses. The post commander at Fort Stanton would in time send a detachment to aid the sheriff in the protection of life and property. Brady controlled the town of Lincoln, but on the night of March 31, 1878, William Bonney, Frank McNab and several other Regulators slipped into the corral behind Tunstall's store. The next morning the unsuspecting sheriff and four deputies were hit by a volley of rifle fire from the corral as they started down the street. Brady fell dead, riddled with bullets, while deputy George Hindman staggered back and then collapsed, mortally wounded. The Regulators disappeared. Three years later it was Bonney who was tried, convicted, and sentenced to hang for Brady's murder.

The sheriff's death cost the Regulators much public sympathy and any real hope of bringing Tunstall's killers to justice. McSween enjoyed a few weeks of victory after one of his people, John Copeland, gained appointment as the interim sheriff. More fateful was the arrival, four days after Brady's death, of Lieutenant Colonel N.A.M. Dudley as the new commandant at Fort Stanton.

That same day a shoot-out at Blazer's Mill on the Mescalero Reservation left both 'Buckshot' Roberts, a member of the posse that killed Tunstall, and Dick Brewer, leader of the Regulators, dead on the ground. Sheriff Copeland dithered until the army pushed him into action, when he arrested one of the Regulators, William Bonney, at Blazer's Mill (modern Ruidoso). Late in April, the Kid skipped out and spent all but a few months of his remaining life dodging the law.

The Dolan and McSween partisans exchanged blow for blow until by the first of June the army estimated that twenty-five men had been killed and all business in Lincoln County had stopped. Lieutenant Colonel Dudley stayed neutral during his first month but then began to show hostility towards McSween's cause. The territorial governor, Samuel Axtell, tipped the odds toward the Dolan faction when he removed John Copeland and appointed George Peppin as sheriff of Lincoln County as of May 28th. For the next month, the troops from Fort Stanton aided Sheriff Peppin while the Regulators continued, with no success, trying to serve their own magistrate warrants for assaults and murders. More outlaws flocked in and terrorized citizens fled the county.

Letters from Lincoln County reached Washington, DC and even London, and got attention in both capitals. Two investigators, Frank Warner Angel from the Department of Justice, and U.S. Indian Inspector E.C. Watkins were dispatched. They collected numerous testimonies, then tried to make sense of it all. Angel penned a vivid report that strongly favored his fellow attorney, while the more seasoned Watkins came back disgusted with McSween. In the meantime, late in June the U.S. army issued new orders that virtually prohibited using troops to aid civil authorities. With the military suddenly on the sidelines, Sheriff Peppin was thrown back on his own resources. Any moderating influence in Lincoln County had just disappeared.

McSween left Lincoln again about June 24th after his name was entered on the sheriff's "wanted" list, thanks to two dead horses that might have been shot by anyone. By now the other Regulators had been named in federal or territorial arrest warrants or both. For three weeks the lawyer and his supporters skirmished with Sheriff Peppin's possemen, now augmented by John Kinney's band of thugs and cattle thieves from down in Doña Ana County. Then on July 14th the running stopped. Just after dark, Alexander McSween led his private army of some forty-five gunmen back to Lincoln, apparently determined to hold his ground and fight it out. Peppin, in Lincoln with his own smaller force, was caught by surprise. He quickly recovered and effectively laid siege to his opponents.

The Lincoln County War reached its climax with the Five-Days Battle in Lincoln, July 15-19, 1878. The fugitive attorney and a dozen men defended his own home, a ten or twelve-room adobe west of the Tunstall store. His wife Susan, her sister and husband and their five children were with him as well. Other supporters occupied the Montaño, Patron, and Ellis stores farther east; Dolan and the sheriff deployed their forces at the old torreon, the Wortley Hotel and nearby homes, all within easy gunshot of the McSween residence.

For three days the two sides blazed away intermittently, the only casualty being one Charlie Crawford, alias 'Lallacooler', mortally wounded by a McSween marksman. Most citizens had fled, but Saturnino Baca huddled in a small house next to the torreon with his family, while bullets flew in all directions. Late on the fourth day, Baca sent a frantic plea for help to Fort Stanton. That evening Dudley conferred with his officers. They decided to march for Lincoln the next morning, to preserve the lives of women and children.

Dudley led his column into Lincoln late in the morning of the fifth day and went into camp opposite the Montaño store. By training a howitzer on the door of the store, he encouraged McSween's partisans to vacate the building. Other supporters left the Patron and Ellis houses . The lawyer soon found himself reduced to a single stronghold, his own home. Gunfire increased and the soldiers took cover, holding their own fire. The men in the sheriff's posse set a fire at one corner of the McSween house and the burning progressed slowly from room to room through the afternoon. In an acrimonious debate with Susan McSween, Dudley claimed that he could not interfere with civil authorities. Later in the day, hostilities were suspended briefly while Mrs. McSween with her sister and the five terrified children were escorted from the burning structure.

As darkness fell and the house blazed, Billy Bonney, the "Kid," reportedly took command. He and five others dashed from the building and dodged a storm of bullets as they raced for the nearby Rio Bonito and disappeared into the brush. They lost only one man. A second group, which included the attorney, delayed too long and were trapped at the back of the yard. Everyone commenced to shoot and the lawyer fell with five bullets in him, while three others died in the same burst of gunfire. The Big Killing, as one witness termed it, ended then. Dudley and his troopers had watched it all.

Civil authority disappeared and outlaw bands overran the country. In a major rout, Sheriff Peppin took refuge at Fort Stanton while William Bonney and other survivors of McSween's ring now held Lincoln. Frank Angel returned to Washington late in August and made his report, with the result that Governor Axtell was promptly removed. In Lincoln County worse was to come when John Selman's "Wrestlers," a particularly vicious group of desperadoes, plundered houses, shot several young boys and added rapes to their existing crimes. Susan McSween remained in Lincoln until September 17 to salvage what she could of her husband's property. By October the violence had run its course and a new governor, Lew. Wallace, tried to smooth the very troubled waters. Lieutenant Colonel Dudley received orders reversing the old restrictions on the military aiding in civilian law enforcement, while in Lincoln a general election saw new county officials voted into office. The district judge nonetheless refused to hold the fall term of court there. In Santa Fe, alcohol claimed the life of Lawrence G. Murphy. He was only forty-five.

Susan McSween returned to Lincoln in November, accompanied by her lawyer, Huston Chapman, to settle the Tunstall and McSween estates. Chapman's conduct soon reminded people of Susan's late husband, and when gunfire echoed again on Lincoln's only street the night of February 18, 1879, the new attorney lay dead in the dirt. This marked the last violent episode of the Lincoln County War. James Dolan and a newly-arrived hard case, Billy Campbell, were accused of the murder. The Fort Stanton commander promptly sent troops and an uneasy peace prevailed.

The Chapman shooting brought Governor Wallace to Lincoln, where he declared a general pardon for misdemeanors and offences against territorial laws. William Bonney, the "Kid," was still on the run but becoming much better known. With the April term of district court now approaching, Wallace convinced Bonney to surrender and turn state's evidence against Campbell and Dolan. The Kid did so, but when the grand jury returned 200 indictments, one was against him for the murders of Sheriff Brady and his deputy. The young outlaw remained in custody until the night of June 17, 1879, when he slipped out of Lincoln and disappeared. Most of the others indicted either pled the governor's pardon, had their cases dismissed, skipped the country, or were tried and found not guilty. Lieutenant Colonel Dudley underwent a military court of inquiry in which nearly all of the survivors testified, but that court adjourned on July 5, 1879 after its board found that none of the allegations of misconduct against him had been sustained. Charges against the same officer in civilian courts were also cleared, and he went on to a prominent role in a new war, this one against the Apache Indian chief, Victorio.

William Bonney was heard from only occasionally until December of 1880, when Sheriff Pat Garrett captured him in a shootout at Stinking Springs, east of Fort Sumner, New Mexico. For all of the murders, thefts and destruction in the Lincoln County War, the only person tried, convicted and sentenced was William Bonney, Billy the Kid, and this for the murder of Sheriff Brady three years earlier. Not surprisingly, he felt singled out. One witness claimed that forty-two men had died of "lead fever," but the total was probably much higher.

Billy the Kid played a moderately important but not a crucial role in the Lincoln County War. The course of the violence would have been the same had he never been present. Events shaped him rather than the other way around. Had there been no Lincoln County War, there would have been no Billy the Kid, and William Bonney would have been known as one more minor outlaw. But even in his own day he had a media appeal, and his death in 1881 was noted in newspapers across the country and even in England. In the view of posterity he has come to dominate the War, and in the many images he has borne since then his personality still grips the popular imagination.

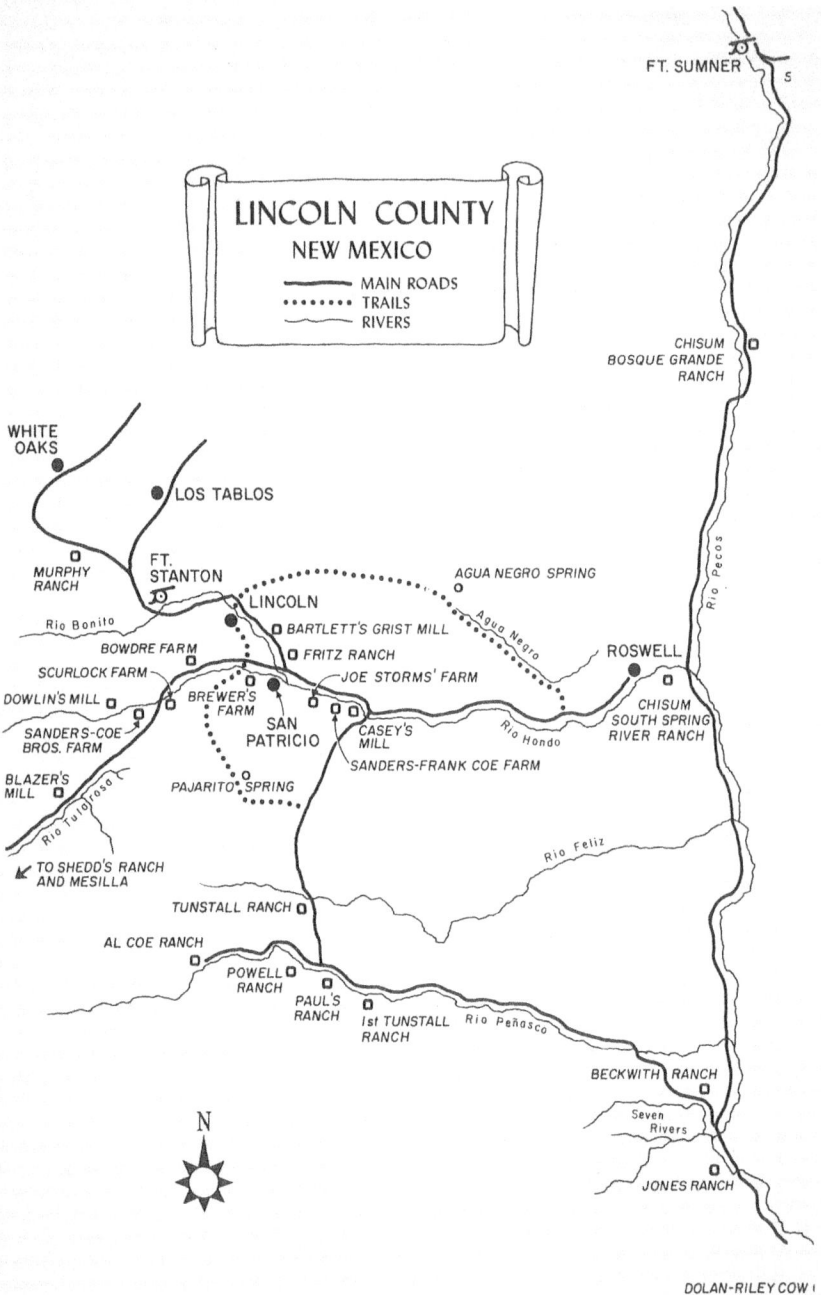

22. Lincoln County, New Mexico, c. 1878. Courtesy Robert N. Mullin, 1968.

Ellis' mill house

Ellis & Sons store

Santo Campo

Rio Bonito

E
N S
W

Site of pit carcel (1st jail)

Juan Patron house & store

Zamora (Rita) home

José Montaño house & store

Ramon Luna home

Gallegos house

Site of Saturnino Baca home

Convento
(1st Courthouse & Wilson's Saloon)

Torreon

San Juan Church

Site of Squire Wilson house

Tunstall store

Site of McSween house

Dolan house

Fresquez house

Ramsey store

Watson house

Wright Annex (formerly a drug store, winery & movie house)

Aragon house

Dr. Wood's house

Zamora home & Aragon store

Wortley Hotel

First school house

Maes Museum & La Paloma Bar

Sheriff Brent house

1921 schoolhouse

George Peppin house

Murphy-Dolan store

NEW MEXICO
STATE
MONUMENT
at
LINCOLN

Buildings of
Historical Importance

Lincoln County
War Period

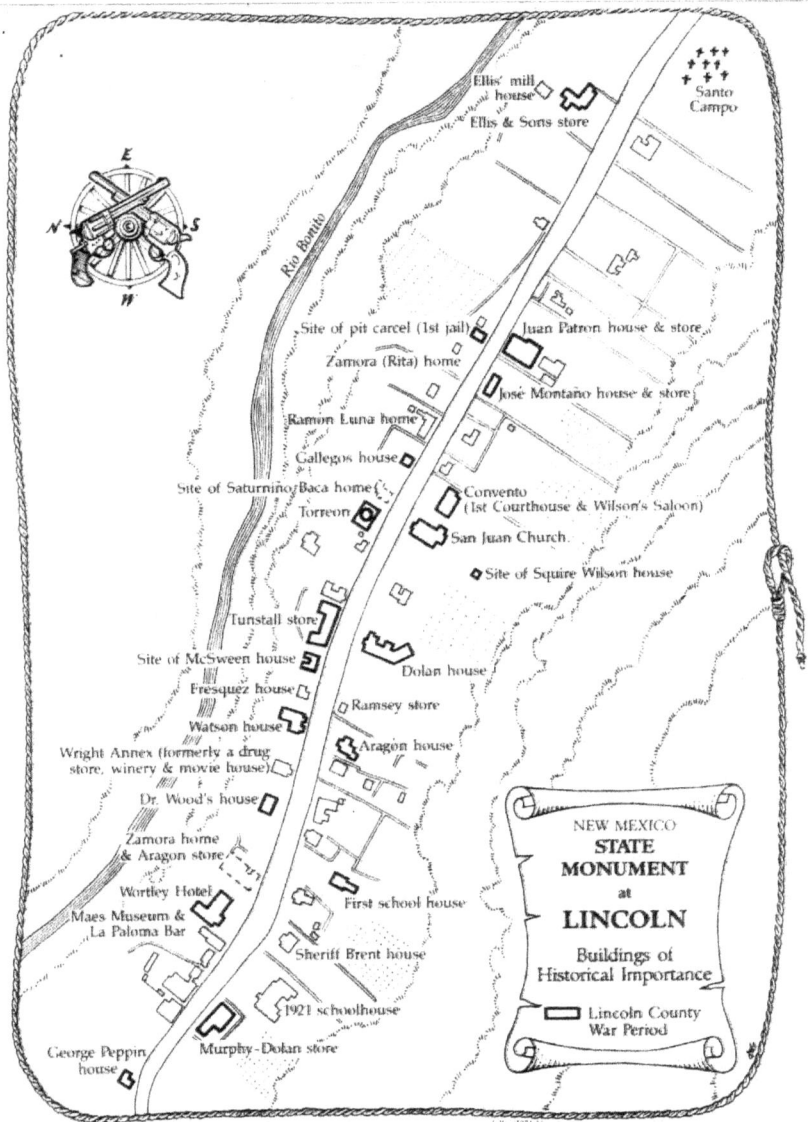

23. Town of Lincoln. Courtesy of New Mexico State Planning Office report, 1974.

REFERENCES

Edwards, Harold L. *Goodbye Billy the Kid.* College Station, Texas: Creative Publishing Company (1995).

Nolan, Frederick, *The Lincoln County War: A Documentary History.* Norman: University of Oklahoma Press (2002).

Utley, Robert M. *High Noon in Lincoln.* Albuquerque: University of New Mexico Press (1987).

Wilson, John P. *Merchants, Guns, & Money.* Santa Fe: Museum of New Mexico Press (1987).

————. "Building His Own Legend: Billy the Kid and the Media." *New Mexico Historical Review,* Vol. 82 #2, pp. 221-235 (Spring 2007).

~ 11 ~

THE ESCAPE OF "THE KID" RECONSIDERED

In its May 11, 1881 issue, the Santa Fe *Daily New Mexican* included the following intriguing paragraph regarding Billy the Kid:

"Newman's Semi-Weekly gives a long account of the Kid and his career, which is not very complimentary to the subject of the story. Some of the incidents narrated are thrilling enough for a dime novel."[1]

If the writer only knew how prophetic his words would be.

Followers of Billy the Kid in recent times can only regret that there is no known surviving copy of the Las Cruces, New Mexico paper, titled variously Newman's Semi-Weekly, Newman's Thirty-Four, and by several other names, beyond the April 20, 1881 number. The account referred to, now lost, must have appeared in an issue between late April and early May. The paper itself continued until sometime in late July, as shown by quotations from it that appeared in exchange newspapers. After this, the proprietor changed the name again and removed his place of publication to nearby El Paso, Texas. The only hope for finding a version of this story is probably as a reprint in another newspaper as yet undiscovered. In its extant issues, Newman's publication regularly reported the Kid's activities.

One "lost" account from Newman's Semi-Weekly *did* appear as a reprint, in the May 14, 1881 *Supplement* to *The New Southwest and Grant County Herald,* a new title in Silver City, New Mexico.[2] The issue of Newman's journal that published this article originally was not cited, but it obviously appeared after the young outlaw's escape from the Lincoln County Courthouse on April 28, 1881. The article itself was mostly about his escape and while published anonymously, a guess as to its author is Sam Corbet, a regular source on events in Lincoln at this period.

In his book *Billy the Kid: A Short and Violent Life,* historian Robert Utley considered this and many other sources in his reconstruction of the April 28th drama in Lincoln.[3] Utley's analysis was thorough and he gave special weight to seemingly firsthand sources, especial the White Oaks, New Mexico *Golden Era* of May 5, 1881 (as reprinted in the *White Oaks Eagle,* February 14, 1901); the account in the Silver City paper on May 14, 1881; Godfrey Gauss' description in the *Lincoln County Leader,* March 1, 1890; and John P. Meadows' recollection in his 1936 newspaper article.[4] While written in the fall of 1881, Sheriff Pat Garrett's account is a second-hand one.[5] Frederick Nolan, biographer of Billy the Kid, was mostly caught up in his own theories as to what may have happened at the courthouse, and less inclined to rely on source materials.[6]

The Gauss and Meadows accounts were written long after the events. The White Oaks version, while contemporary, is actually second-hand. Lincoln at the time had no newspaper. As Utley concluded, these circumstances have left the Silver City paper's article, which is both contemporary and first-hand, deserving of special mention. It was highly descriptive, well-written and included details not found elsewhere. The only public access to a copy has been via an old University of New Mexico Library microfilm of *The New Southwest and Grant County Herald* (1881–1882). Sam Corbet should have been a reliable witness. The misspellings are in the original.

The following letter, originally published in *Newman's Semi Weekly,* furnishes the particulars of the escape of Henry McCarty, *alias,* Henry Antrin, *alias,* Billy Bonney, *alias* "The Kid," who was convicted of murder in the first degree, at the last Mesilla term of court, and had been taken to Lincoln county to be executed.

Lincoln, N.M., April 20.

Dear Sir:

Kid killed his guard, Bob Olinger and deputy Sheriff J.W. Bell, last night and made his escape. It happened as follows:

Kid was kept as a prisoner in the southeast corner room of the Murphy building. He had on the shackles and handcuffs he wore when he came here. The handcuffs were off from one hand and his hands were really free. Bob Olinger left about 6 p.m. to go to supper and left Kid alone with Bell. He and the others who went to supper had just got into Sam Wortley's place and sat down to the table when they heard three shots fired from the building. Bob Olinger jumping up from the table, said "they are having a fight over there," started in the lead and ran over to the building. Just as he entered the gate Kid discharged Olinger's double-barreled shot gun at him, delivering the contents of both barrels into his head and breast, killing him instantly, and Olinger fell right in front of the post office door, the office occupied by Ben Ellis.

It seems Kid had struck Bell over the head with the handcuffs and back of the ear also, breaking his skull and stunning him and then grabbing from Bell his revolver; and Bell, after partially recovering from the effects of the blow, started to run out of the hall and down stairs and Kid fired a shot at him which passed under Bell's arms and clear through his body. Bell ran towards the kitchen and old man Goss was just coming out of it and Bell fell into his arms and expired without a word.

Ellis and myself had started for supper before Olinger and the others had left. We board at Rob Ellis' father's, and had got down the street as far as La Rue's store when we heard firing. As I looked back I thought the smoke came from west of the building and that perhaps it was some Mexicans firing up above the office and paid no attention to it but went on to supper.

After we had returned and got to Captain Baca's we learned what had been done. Kid was then on the porch of the building with Olinger's shot gun, a Winchester and two revolvers, holding the fort and keeping any person from going to town, saying he would shoot the first man who started to give any alarm. He leveled the Winchester on old man Goss and made him saddle a pony that was in the corral and go into my room and take the blankets off from the bed.

Pat Garrett had stored arms which he had taken from the Tularosa prisoners, four guns and four revolvers. Kid broke the door in and took two revolvers, four belts of cartridges, and a new Winchester.

When Goss led the horse out of the corral he let him go, and Kid ordered Nunnelly, one of the prisoners, to catch him and return him and help him on. He had broken one shackle on his leg; so his legs were free, except the chain and shackle was yet attached to the one leg.

It was more than an hour, after he killed Olinger and Bell, before he left. He had at his command eight revolvers and six guns. He stood on the upper porch in front of the building and talked with the people who were in Wortley's, but would not let anyone come towards him. He told the people that he did not want to kill Bell but, as he ran, he had to. He said he grabbed Bell's revolver and told him to hold up his hands and surrender; that Bell started to run and he had to kill him. He declared he was "standing pat" against the world; and, while he did not wish to kill anybody, if anybody interfered with his attempt to escape he would kill him.

After he had got all ready to leave the building he took Bob Olinger's double-barreled shot gun and broke it into pieces by striking it across the railing of the porch and then threw the pieces down on Olinger's dead body and said "here is your gun, G—d d—n you! You won't follow me with it any longer." He then took off his handcuffs and threw them at the dead body of Bell, saying "here, G--d d--n you! Take them! I guess you won't put them on me again.

Just at dark he mounted and rode to a Mexican house a few hundred yards off and bought a rope and said "Boys, I don't know these mountains," and started off through the bottom and struck for the Capitans. It is said he made violent threats against those whom he considers have injured him and that he said he did not consider he had been bad heretofore but would let people know hereafter what it is to be a bad man. When he rode off, he went on a walk, and every act, from beginning to end, seemed to have been placed and executed with the coolest deliberation.

I have understood that he had said he would give Judge Bristol, Judge Newcomb and Colonel Rynerson a round up; but so many things are being told of him that it is hard to tell what he has said.

The old feeling of dread and fear has come back upon us again and it is hard to tell what the end will be. At the time this occurred, Sheriff Garret was at White Oaks on a collecting tour. The Sheriff and his *posse* have been warned time and again about using the utmost caution, but no avail. Only two days ago Olinger left his revolver loose on the table in front of Kid, and if a person had not taken it Kid would then undoubtedly have made a break. I have several times cautioned Olinger and he has replied that, as far as Kid's getting away was concerned, he had just as soon he had on no irons—he could not get away from him. His over-confidence in himself has been the means of his own destruction, as well as robbing the gallows of its victim. It is a great misfortune and one that will tell seriously against us. I have about abandoned the hope that Lincoln will ever come out of her condition of lawlessness.

24. Lincoln County Courthouse, c. 1886. R.G. McCubbin collection.

25. Billy the Kid. From *History of New Mexico, Its Resources and People,* Vol. 1, 1907 by George B. Anderson.

NOTES

1. *The Daily New Mexican*, May 11, 1881, p. 4 Col. 1.

2. *Supplement to The New Southwest and Grant County Herald*, May 14, 1881, p. 1 cols. 1-2.

3. Utley, Robert M. *Billy the Kid: A Short and Violent Life*. Lincoln: University of Nebraska Press (1989), pp. 179-185, 261-265.

4. *White Oaks Eagle*, February 14, 1901, as transcribed by Edith L. Crawford, New Mexico WPA records; *Lincoln County Leader*, March 1, 1890; John P. Wilson, *Pat Garrett and Billy the Kid As I Knew Them; Reminiscences of John P, Meadows*. Albuquerque: University of New Mexico Press (2004), pp. 47-51.

5. Garrett, Pat F. *The Authentic Life of Billy the Kid*. Santa Fe: New Mexican Printing and Publishing Co. (1882). New Edition. Santa Fe: Sunstone Press (2007)

6. Nolan, Frederick. *The West of Billy the Kid*. Norman: University of Oklahoma Press (1998), pp. 271-277, 323-324

~ 12 ~

FAITHFUL SHEP HOLDS THE FORT

ONE OF THE MOST DESOLATE LOCATIONS ALONG THE BUTTERFIELD OVERLAND Mail's early route across western Texas lay at Crow Spring, in a salt pan known as Crow Flats, ninety-four miles by road east of El Paso. The station here, a mile south of the New Mexico line, had been built mostly of adobe and gypsum blocks. It served for scarcely a year, then slowly fell into ruin after the mail line began to follow a more southerly route in 1859.

In January 1880 two young men from Denver, J.P. Andrews and W.P. Wiswald, stopped to make dinner in the shelter of the old walls. They had set out from Ysleta, a dozen miles below El Paso on the Rio Grande, to seek opportunities in the Pecos River Valley some 150 miles to the east. Their equipment included a new ambulance (a light carriage), two good horses and a saddle pony, with plenty of grub and arms. A big black shepard dog named Shep accompanied them. The trip coincided with a peak period of Apache chief Victorio's raiding across southern New Mexico and far western Texas.

At Crow Spring, the men turned their team out to graze. Suddenly they heard yelling and the trampling of horses' hooves; looking up, they saw four or five Indians driving off their animals. The travelers grabbed their guns and started after the thieves on foot, but some of the raiders fought to delay pursuit while others got away with the horses. Back at the old station, now afoot and chilled by a cold north wind, the two companions decided to seek help from along the Pecos.

They pushed their ambulance and other property inside the ruined walls and rigged up two dummy sentinels, then set out after midnight. Shep wanted to go too, but they put a sack of corn and a side of bacon under the ambulance and made him understand that he was to stay and guard it.

By the next evening the travelers found themselves south of Guadalupe Peak and abruptly facing an entire village of Apaches, who were headed towards them. Everyone recovered from their surprise and a sharp fight broke out. The two men wounded one warrior, then took off running back towards Crow Flats as night fell. They made it back safely. Their dummy sentinels still stood guard and the faithful shepard dog was overjoyed at the return of his masters.

After resting the next day they decided to pull out for El Paso. Their shoes were now worn out and they tied their feet up in gunny sacks. Once again Shep received his orders. Not so much as a cow camp lay between them and Hueco Tanks, a small ranch twenty-four miles east of El Paso that marked the last settlement going east.

Andrews and Wiswald found no help at El Paso, so the weary men trudged down to the Texas Ranger camp at Ysleta. The small Ranger company there formed part of the Frontier Battalion. In those days, the Texas Rangers pursued lawbreakers, trailed and fought with hostile Indians, and aided citizens in trouble. The Ranger Lieutenant decided to represent the honor and dignity of Texas by setting off with eight Rangers and a guide to accompany the two Denverites back to their ambulance.

For four days they retraced the old Butterfield Trail east from Hueco Tanks, until finally the twelve-man party rode the last twenty-eight miles to Crow Flats and arrived in the night. There to challenge them was the ever-watchful guardian, old Shep. According to the Ranger Lieutenant, George Wythe Baylor,

> "…when he [Shep] heard his master's voice he went wild with joy, barked, rolled over, stood on his head [?], …and we gave him a cheer. He had been there alone for fifteen days. His side of bacon was eaten, and the sack of corn [was] getting very low. The Rangers were as much delighted as if it had been a human being they had rescued."

Shep had worn the top of the remaining station walls perfectly smooth by his pacing, while keeping out the coyotes. Their tracks were thick all around, but Shep and the dummy sentinels had held the fort. Everything was just as the owners had left it.

Everyone then returned safely to Ysleta, although preceded by a rumor that the entire party has been massacred. The Texas Ranger Lieutenant and his sergeant agreed that Shep's valiant defense merited a monument in the plaza at El Paso.

26. Overland Mail coach at Crow Flats. Courtesy of www.TexasHistory.com

REFERENCES

Conkling, Roscoe P. and Margaret B. *The Butterfield Overland Mail 1857–1869,* Vol. I. Glendale, California: The Arthur H. Clark Co. (1947).

Gerow, Peggy A. *Along the Butterfield Trail II.* Albuquerque: Office of Contract Archeology, University of New Mexico (1996).

Gillett, James B. *Six Years With The Texas Rangers 1875 to 1881,* Chapter 18. Chicago: The Lakeside Press (1943). Reprint of 1925 edition.

Baylor, George Wythe (edited by Jerry D. Thompson), *Into The Far, Wild Country,* Chapter Six (pp. 292-298). El Paso: Texas Western Press (1996). The quotation is from this volume.

~ 13 ~

THE RANGER AND THE SABOTEUR

We think of the sheriffs and U.S. Marshals of the Old West as the men who brought law to the mesquite in early-day New Mexico. But what about up in the ponderosas, among the mountain valleys, widely-scattered ranches, small farms, and thousands of sheep that grazed in the pine-shadowed forest lands? There, such duties often fell to the Forest Rangers who tended the Forest Reserves and later the National Forests.

Elliott Barker had a long and distinguished career as an author, poet, and for twenty-two years as Director of the New Mexico Department of Game and Fish. In the latter days of World War 1 he served as Forest Supervisor on Carson National Forest. One day in 1918 he received a phone call from Santa Fe, telling him that a man named Alex Nagy, an enemy alien (the name is Hungarian), armed and probably dangerous, was thought to be at the old Maupin Ranch west of Tres Piedras. Barker was tasked to arrest him. In his later recollections, the ranger said that Nagy had supposedly burned grain silos in Kansas and damaged farmlands in the Estancia Valley. In other words, he was a saboteur.

In that era, burning wheat fields and silos was a perfectly legitimate form of sabotage. But this man wasn't your everyday enemy agent. Germany and Austria-Hungary fought together in World War I as the Central Powers, against France, Great Britain, Italy and the United States. Alexander Nagy appears to have been an exotic specimen, one who worked for the government of the Austro-Hungarian Emperor, Franz Josef the First, instead of the German Kaiser.

Elliot Barker was a deputy U.S. Marshal as well as a Forest Supervisor, and he made his way to the Maupin ranch with Ranger E.L. Perry, armed and forewarned. According to the Carson National Forest newsletter, the *Carson Bulletin*, Nagy had gotten himself in trouble by impersonating a Forest Service officer. He posed as such at Amador's store in Vallecitos, and also at Cañon Plaza a few miles above Vallecitos, where he issued what purported to be a free-use permit to Juan C. Gurule to cut twenty-five pine poles or house logs.

Barker rode down from the San Antonio Ranger Station some thirty miles distant and was waiting near the Maupin ranch on the morning of September 1, 1918. Shortly after daylight, the rancher and the man being sought came out of the house. When they started down into a nearby oat field, the Forest Supervisor rode up and called them over. The two were unarmed. When asked his name, the man gave it and proved to be the person Barker was looking for. The ranger showed them his authority as a deputy marshal and told them he had orders to take Nagy in.

The enemy agent made no protest, but rancher Roy Maupin argued vigorously that he just wouldn't let him go, that help was hard to get and he was sure the fellow was all right. Barker said that the judge would decide whether the man was all right or not. Maupin kept it up until the marshal finally snapped out that if he didn't shut up and let him carry out his orders, he would take both of them in and they could walk ahead of him in the road all the way. The ranch lay about eight miles west of Tres Piedras, New Mexico. Maupin finally conceded "Maybe you're right, maybe that's the authority."

Nagy asked if he could go to the house and get his coat and some other things that he had there. Barker replied, "Yes, I will go with you." Mrs. Maupin was getting breakfast as they walked into the kitchen. The ranger paused to say "Good morning, Mrs. Maupin. I have a little business with this man here," then started to follow him up the steep, narrow stairway that led to a landing opposite Nagy's sleeping room. When the agent started to hurry, Barker did too, but he had on chaps and spurs as well as his gun belt.

At the top of the landing, the door to the room stood open and the fellow was throwing his coat off the bed with one hand and grabbing something with the other. Barker knew instantly that this must be a gun and, quick as anything, "I drew my gun and stuck it right in his kidneys and said 'Drop it you son-of-a-so-and-so, or I'll kill you!" Nagy half-turned around with his .45 cocked, but then dropped it to the floor. It struck but didn't go off. The ranger-lawman had acted just in the nick of time and his own six-gun got all of the attention necessary.

Barker took the saboteur to Tres Piedras, where a U.S. Commissioner came up from Taos on September 2nd and held a preliminary hearing. He bound Nagy over to await the action of a Federal district court. While being brought back to Taos by the commissioner pending the arrival of a U.S. Marshal, Nagy escaped. He was rearrested at Española the following day and taken to Santa Fe. The September newspapers in Santa Fe and Albuquerque carried no notice of these events although they reported at length on Allied advances in France.

The criminal case file for Alexander Nagy, now in the Denver Federal Records Center, states that he stood trial in Albuquerque on December 22, 1918, the only charge being unlawfully pretending to be a Forest Ranger and granting permission to cut timber on a National Forest. He was found not guilty. Nothing in his file said anything about him being an enemy alien.

According to Barker, however, Nagy was sent to the penitentiary for the duration of the war while the ranger kept the .45 as a souvenir, only to have it stolen years later. He left the Forest Service and turned to ranching, until one day the agent, now out of prison, had the gall to write and say he wanted his gun back! Barker replied that if he thought he was man enough, to come and get it. No one showed up.

Unfortunately, while the master alien registration records for the World War I period might have documented any actions involving Nagy, these were destroyed in 1922. Upon my inquiry, the Kansas State Historical Society could find no mention of an Alexander Nagy. An Internet search revealed no specific results as this was an extremely common name.

Elliott Barker enjoyed a very long life, from his birth in Texas on Christmas Day in 1886 to his death in Santa Fe on Easter Sunday in 1988. The Forest Service did not want or expect its rangers to be gunslingers, and only this once did he draw his gun on anybody. From 1931 to 1953 he directed the New Mexico Department of Game and Fish while writing poetry and such wildlife classics as *Beatty's Cabin* and *When the Dogs Barked 'Treed'*. Then in 1950, firefighters rescued an angry little bear cub with singed paws, "Hot Foot Teddy," from a fire in the Capitan Mountains. The Game and Fish director donated him to the U.S. Forest Service. The cub went to Washington and the National Zoo, there to become the symbol of forest fire prevention as Smokey Bear.

27. World War I patriotic poster. Library of Congress collections.

REFERENCES

Carson Bulletin, September 9, 1918.

NARA Denver Federal Center, District of New Mexico Criminal Case Files 1912-53, Case #1213.

The Early Days: A Sourcebook of Southwestern Region History, Book 1, compiled by Edwin A. Tucker. USDA Forest Service Southwestern Region, Cultural Resources Management Report No. 7 (September 1989). Albuquerque, New Mexico.

Janis L. Wiggins, Archivist, NARA College Park, Maryland, January 9, 2003, to John P. Wilson.

William Grace, Kansas State Historical Society, Topeka, February 7, 2003, to John P Wilson.

An earlier version of this chapter appeared in *Sunshine and Shadows in New Mexico's Past*. Vol. III (2012). Los Ranchos: Rio Grande Books.

SUGGESTED READINGS

Alberts, Don E. *Rebels on the Rio Grande: The Civil War Journal of A.B. Peticolas.* Albuquerque: University of New Mexico Press, 1984.

All Trails Lead to Santa Fe: An Anthology Commemorating the 400th Anniversary of the Founding of Santa Fe, New Mexico, in 1610. Santa Fe: Sunstone Press, 2010.

Bolton, Herbert Eugene. *Coronado: Knight of Pueblos and Plains.* Albuquerque: University of New Mexico Press, 1949.

Eidenbach, Peter L. *An Atlas of Historic New Mexico Maps 1540–1941.* Albuquerque: University of New Mexico Press, 2012

Garrett, Pat F. *The Authentic Life of Billy, The Kid.* New Edition, Santa Fe: Sunstone Press, 2007.

Hendricks, Rick. *New Mexico in 1801: The Priests Report.* Los Ranchos de Albuquerque: Rio Grande Books, 2008.

Hendricks, Rick, and John P. Wilson. *The Navajos in 1705.* Albuquerque: University of New Mexico Press, 1996.

Kessell, John L. *Kiva, Cross, and Crown: The Pecos Indians and New Mexico, 1540–1840*. Washington: National Park Service, 1979.

Kessell, John L. *Spain in the Southwest: A Narrative History of Colonial New Mexico, Arizona, Texas, and California*. Norman: University of Oklahoma Press, 2002.

Melzer, Richard, editor. *Sunshine and Shadows in New Mexico's Past, Volumes I, II, and III*. Historical Society of New Mexico. Los Ranchos: Rio Grande Press, 2010, 2011, 2012.

New Mexico Historical Review: Special Spanish Colonial Era Issue (Volume 64 No. 3). Albuquerque, July 1989.

Noble, David Grant, editor. *Santa Fe: History of an Ancient City*. Santa Fe: School of Advanced Research Press, 2008.

Otero, Miguel Antonio. *The Real Billy the Kid*. New Edition, Santa Fe: Sunstone Press, 2006.

Simmons, Marc. *Coronado's Land: Essays on Daily Life in Colonial New Mexico*. Albuquerque: University of New Mexico Press, 1991.

Simmons, Marc. *Stalking Billy the Kid: Brief Sketches of a Short Life*. Santa Fe: Sunstone Press, 2006.

Utley, Robert M. *Billy the Kid: A Short and Violent Life*. Lincoln: University of Nebraska Press, 1989.

Whitford, William Clarke. *Colorado Volunteers in the Civil War: The New Mexico Campaign in 1862*. Boulder: Pruett Press Inc., 1963.

Williams, Jerry L., and Paul E. McCallister, editors. *New Mexico in Maps*. Albuquerque: University of New Mexico Press, 1979.

Wilson, John P. *Merchants, Guns, and Money: The Story of Lincoln County and Its Wars*. Santa Fe: Museum of New Mexico Press, 1987.

www.ingramcontent.com/pod-product-compliance
Lightning Source LLC
Chambersburg PA
CBHW031141090426
42738CB00008B/1175